B O O K   1

English

No Problem!

Trish Kerns
Old Marshall Adult Education Center
Sacramento City Unified School District, CA

Patty Long
Old Marshall Adult Education Center
Sacramento City Unified School District, CA

New Readers Press

English—No Problem!™
English—No Problem! Level 1 Student Book
ISBN 1-56420-356-5

Copyright © 2004 New Readers Press
New Readers Press
Division of ProLiteracy Worldwide
1320 Jamesville Avenue, Syracuse, New York 13210
www.newreaderspress.com

Printed in the United States of America
9   8   7   6   5   4   3   2

All proceeds from the sale of New Readers Press materials support literacy programs in the United States and worldwide.

Acquisitions Editor: Paula L. Schlusberg
Developer: Mendoza and Associates
Project Director: Roseanne Mendoza
Project Editor: Pat Harrington-Wydell
Content Editor: Terrie Lipke
Production Director: Heather Witt-Badoud
Designer: Kimbrly Koennecke
Illustrations: Carolyn Boehmer, Matt Terry, Linda Tiff, James Wallace
Production Specialist: Alexander Jones
Cover Design: Kimbrly Koennecke
Photo Credits: Hal Silverman Studio, Dave Revette Photography
Cover Photography: Robert Mescavage Photography

Authors

Trish Kerns
Old Marshall Adult Education Center
Sacramento City Unified
  School District, CA

Patty Long
Old Marshall Adult Education Center
Sacramento City Unified
  School District, CA

Contributors

National Council Members
Audrey Abed, *San Marcos Even Start Program, San Marcos, TX*
Myra K. Baum, *New York City Board of Education (retired), New York, NY*
Kathryn Hamilton, *Elk Grove Adult and Community Education, Sacramento, CA*
Brigitte Marshall, *Oakland Adult Education Programs, Oakland, CA*
Teri McLean, *Florida Human Resources Development Center, Gainesville, FL*
Alan Seaman, *Wheaton College, Wheaton, IL*

Reviewers
Sabrina Budasi-Martin, *William Rainey Harper College, Palatine, IL*
Linda Davis-Pluta, *Oakton Community College, Des Plaines, IL*
Patricia DeHesus-Lopez, *Center for Continuing Education, Texas A&M University,*
  Kingsville, TX
Gail Feinstein Forman, *San Diego City College, San Diego, CA*
Carolyn Harding, *Marshall High School Adult Program, Falls Church, VA*
Debe Pack-Garcia, *Manteca Adult School, Humbolt, CA*
Lydia Omori, *William Rainey Harper College, Palatine, IL*
Pamela Patterson, *Seminole Community College, Sanford, FL*
Catherine Porter, *Adult Learning Resource Center, Des Plaines, IL*
Jean Rose, *ABC Adult School, Cerritos, CA*
Eric Rosenbaum, *Bronx Community College Adult Program, Bronx, NY*
Laurie Shapero, *Miami-Dade Community College, Miami, FL*
Terry Shearer, *North Harris College Community Education, Houston, TX*
Abigail Tom, *Durham Technical Community College, Chapel Hill, NC*
Darla Wickard, *North Harris College Community Education, Houston, TX*

Pilot Teachers
Connie Bateman, *Gerber Adult Education Center, Sacramento, CA*
Jennifer Bell, *William Rainey Harper College, Palatine, IL*
Marguerite Bock, *Chula Vista Adult School, Chula Vista, CA*
Giza Braun, *National City Adult School, National City, CA*
Sabrina Budasi-Martin, *William Rainey Harper College, Palatine, IL*
Wong-Ling Chew, *Citizens Advice Bureau, Bronx, NY*
Renee Collins, *Elk Grove Adult and Community Education, Sacramento, CA*
Rosette Dawson, *North Harris College Community Education, Houston, TX*
Kathleen Edel, *Elk Grove Adult and Community Education, Sacramento, CA*
Margaret Erwin, *Elk Grove Adult and Community Education, Sacramento, CA*
Teresa L. Gonzalez, *North Harris College Community Education, Houston, TX*
Fernando L. Herbert, *Bronx Adult School, Bronx, NY*
Carolyn Killean, *North Harris College Community Education, Houston, TX*
Elizabeth Minicz, *William Rainey Harper College, Palatine, IL*
Larry Moore, *Long Beach Adult School, Long Beach, CA*
Lydia Omori, *William Rainey Harper College, Palatine, IL*
Valsa Panikulam, *William Rainey Harper College, Palatine, IL*

Kathryn Powell, *William Rainey Harper College, Palatine, IL*
Alan Reiff, *NYC Board of Education, Adult and Continuing Education, Bronx, NY*
Brenda M. Rodriguez, *San Marcos Even Start Program, San Marcos, TX*
Juan Carlos Rodriguez, *San Marcos Even Start Program, San Marcos, TX*
Joan Siff, *NYC Board of Education, Adult and Continuing Education, Bronx, NY*
Susie Simon, *Long Beach Adult School, Long Beach, CA*
Gina Tauber, *North Harris College, Houston, TX*
Diane Villanueva, *Elk Grove Adult and Community Education, Sacramento, CA*
Dona Wayment, *Elk Grove Adult and Community Education, Sacramento, CA*
Weihua Wen, *NYC Board of Education, Adult and Continuing Education, Bronx, NY*
Darla Wickard, *North Harris College Community Education, Houston, TX*
Judy Wurtz, *Sweetwater Union High School District, Chula Vista, CA*

Focus Group Participants
Leslie Jo Adams, *Laguna Niguel, CA*
Fiona Armstrong, *New York City Board of Education, New York, NY*
Myra K. Baum, *New York City Board of Education (retired), New York, NY*
Gretchen Bitterlin, *San Diego Unified School District, San Diego, CA*
Patricia DeHesus-Lopez, *Center for Continuing Education, Texas A&M University,
  Kingsville, TX*
Diana Della Costa, *Worksite ESOL Programs, Kissimmee, FL*
Frankie Dovel, *Orange County Public Schools, VESOL Program, Orlando, FL*
Marianne Dryden, *Region 1 Education Service Center, Edinburgh, TX*
Richard Firsten, *Lindsay Hopkins Technical Center, Miami, FL*
Pamela S. Forbes, *Bartlett High School, Elgin, IL*
Kathryn Hamilton, *Elk Grove Adult and Community Education, Sacramento, CA*
Trish Kerns, *Old Marshall Adult Education Center, Sacramento City Unified School
  District, Sacramento, CA*
Suzanne Leibman, *The College of Lake County, Grayslake, IL*
Patty Long, *Old Marshall Adult Education Center, Sacramento City Unified School
  District, Sacramento, CA*
Brigitte Marshall, *Oakland Adult Education Programs, Oakland, CA*
Bet Messmer, *Santa Clara Adult School, Santa Clara, CA*
Patricia Mooney, *New York State Board of Education, Albany, NY*
Lee Ann Moore, *Salinas Adult School, Salinas, CA*
Lynne Nicodemus, *San Juan Adult School, Carmichael, CA*
Pamela Patterson, *Seminole Community College, Sanford, FL*
Eric Rosenbaum, *Bronx Community College, Bronx, NY*
Linda Sasser, *Alhambra District Office, Alhambra, CA*
Federico Salas, *North Harris College Community Education, Houston, TX*
Alan Seaman, *Wheaton College, Wheaton, IL*
Kathleen Slattery, *Salinas Adult School, Salinas, CA*
Carol Speigl, *Center for Continuing Education, Texas A&M University, Kingsville, TX*
Edie Uber, *Santa Clara Adult School, Santa Clara, CA*
Lise Wanage, *CASAS, Phoenix, AZ*

Special thanks to Kathryn Hamilton for her help in the development of this book.

About This Series

Meeting Adult Learners' Needs with *English—No Problem!*

English—No Problem! is a theme-based, performance-based series focused on developing critical thinking and cultural awareness and on building language and life skills. Designed for adult and young adult English language learners, the series addresses themes and issues meaningful to adults in the United States.

English—No Problem! is appropriate for and respectful of adult learners. These are some key features:

- interactive, communicative, participatory approach
- rich, authentic language
- problem-posing methodology
- project-based units and task-based lessons
- goal setting embedded in each unit and lesson
- units organized around themes of adult relevance
- contextualized, inductive grammar
- student materials designed to fit into lesson plans
- performance assessment, including tools for learner self-evaluation

Series Themes

Across the series, units have the following themes:

- Life Stages: Personal Growth and Goal Setting
- Making Connections
- Taking Care of Yourself
- Personal Finance
- Consumer Awareness
- Protecting Your Legal Rights
- Participating in Your New Country and Community
- Lifelong Learning
- Celebrating Success

At each level, these themes are narrowed to subthemes that are level-appropriate in content and language.

English—No Problem! Series Components

Five levels make up the series:

- literacy
- level 1 (low beginning)
- level 2 (high beginning)
- level 3 (low intermediate)
- level 4 (high intermediate)

The series includes the following components.

Student Book

A full-color student book is the core of each level of *English—No Problem!* Literacy skills, vocabulary, grammar, reading, writing, listening, speaking, and SCANS-type skills are taught and practiced.

Teacher's Edition

Each teacher's edition includes these tools:

- general suggestions for using the series
- scope and sequence charts for the level
- lesson-specific teacher notes with reduced student book pages
- complete scripts for all listening activities and Pronunciation Targets in the student book

Workbook

A workbook provides contextualized practice in the skills taught at each level. Activities relate to the student book stories. Workbook activities are especially useful for learners working individually.

 This icon in the teacher's edition indicates where workbook activities can be assigned.

Reproducible Masters

The reproducible masters include photocopiable materials for the level. Some masters are unit-specific, such as contextualized vocabulary and grammar activities, games, and activities focusing on higher-level thinking skills. Others are generic graphic organizers. Still other masters can be used by teachers, peers, and learners themselves to assess the work done in each unit.

Each masters book also includes scripts for all listening activities in the masters. (Note: These activities are *not* included on the *English—No Problem!* audio recordings.)

 This icon in the teacher's edition indicates where reproducible masters can be used.

Audio Recording

Available on CD and cassette, each level's audio component includes listening passages, listening activities, and Pronunciation Targets from the student book.

This icon in the student book and teacher's edition indicates that the audio recording includes material for that activity.

Lesson-Plan Builder

This free, web-based *Lesson-Plan Builder* allows teachers to create and save customized lesson plans, related graphic organizers, and selected assessment masters. Goals, vocabulary lists, and other elements are already in the template for each lesson. Teachers then add their own notes to customize their plans. They can also create original graphic organizers using generic templates.

When a lesson plan is finished, the customized materials can be printed and stored in PDF form.

 This icon in the teacher's edition refers teachers to the *Lesson-Plan Builder,* found at www.enp.newreaderspress.com.

Vocabulary Cards

For literacy, level 1, and level 2, all vocabulary from the Picture Dictionaries and Vocabulary boxes in the student books is also presented on reproducible flash cards. At the literacy level, the cards also include capital letters, lowercase letters, and numerals.

Placement Tool

The Placement Test student booklet includes items that measure exit skills for each level of the series so that learners can start work in the appropriate student book. The teacher's guide includes a listening script, as well as guidelines for administering the test to a group, for giving an optional oral test, and for interpreting scores.

Hot Topics in ESL

These online professional development articles by adult ESL experts focus on key issues and instructional techniques embodied in *English—No Problem!,* providing background information to enhance effective use of the materials. They are available online at www.enp.newreaderspress.com.

Addressing the Standards

English—No Problem! has been correlated from the earliest stages of development with national standards for adult education and ESL, including the NRS (National Reporting System), EFF (Equipped for the Future), SCANS (Secretary's Commission on Achieving Necessary Skills), CASAS (Comprehensive Adult Student Assessment System) competencies, BEST (Basic English Skills Test), and SPLs (Student Performance Levels). The series also reflects state standards from New York, California, and Florida.

About the Student Books

Each unit in the student books includes a two-page unit opener followed by three lessons (two at the literacy level). A cumulative unit project concludes each unit. Every unit addresses all four language skills—

listening, speaking, reading, and writing. Each lesson focuses on characters operating in one of the three EFF-defined adult roles—parent/family member at home, worker at school or work, or citizen/community member in the larger community.

Unit Opener Pages

Unit Goals The vocabulary, language, pronunciation, and culture goals set forth in the unit opener correlate to a variety of state and national standards.

Opening Question and Photo The opening question, photo, and caption introduce the unit protagonists and engage learners affectively in issues the unit explores.

Think and Talk This feature of levels 1–4 presents questions based on classic steps in problem-posing methodology, adjusted and simplified as needed.

What's Your Opinion? In levels 1–4, this deliberately controversial question often appears after Think and Talk or on the first page of a lesson. It is designed to encourage lively teacher-directed discussion, even among learners with limited vocabulary.

Picture Dictionary or Vocabulary Box This feature introduces important unit vocabulary and concepts.

Gather Your Thoughts In levels 1–4, this activity helps learners relate the unit theme to their own lives. They record their thoughts in a graphic organizer, following a model provided.

What's the Problem? This activity, which follows Gather Your Thoughts, encourages learners to practice another step in problem posing. They identify a possible problem and apply the issue to their own lives.

Setting Goals This feature of levels 1–4 is the first step of a unit's self-evaluation strand. Learners choose from a list of language and life goals and add their own goal to the list. The goals are related to the lesson activities and tasks and to the unit project. After completing a unit, learners revisit these goals in Check Your Progress, the last page of each workbook unit.

First Lesson Page

While the unit opener sets up an issue or problem, the lessons involve learners in seeking solutions while simultaneously developing language competencies.

Lesson Goals and EFF Role The lesson opener lists language, culture, and life-skill goals and identifies the EFF role depicted in that lesson.

Pre-Reading or Pre-Listening Question This question prepares learners to seek solutions to the issues presented in the reading or listening passage or lesson graphic that follows.

Reading or Listening Tip At levels 1–4, this feature presents comprehension and analysis strategies used by good listeners and readers.

Lesson Stimulus Each lesson starts with a reading passage (a picture story at the literacy level), a listening passage, or a lesson graphic. A photo on the page sets the situation for a listening passage. Each listening passage is included in the audio recording, and scripts are provided at the end of the student book and the teacher's edition. A lesson graphic may be a schedule, chart, diagram, graph, time line, or similar item. The questions that follow each lesson stimulus focus on comprehension and analysis.

Remaining Lesson Pages

Picture Dictionary, Vocabulary Box, and Idiom Watch These features present the active lesson vocabulary. At lower levels, pictures often help convey meaning. Vocabulary boxes for the literacy level also include letters and numbers. At levels 3 and 4, idioms are included in every unit.

Class, Group, or Partner Chat This interactive feature provides a model miniconversation. The model sets up a real-life exchange that encourages use of the lesson vocabulary and grammatical structures. Learners ask highly structured and controlled questions and record classmates' responses in a graphic organizer.

Grammar Talk At levels 1–4, the target grammatical structure is presented in several examples. Following the examples is a short explanation or question that guides learners to come up with a rule on their own. At the literacy level, language boxes highlight basic grammatical structures without formal teaching.

Pronunciation Target In this feature of levels 1–4, learners answer questions that lead them to discover pronunciation rules for themselves.

Chat Follow-Ups Learners use information they recorded during the Chat activity. They write patterned sentences, using lesson vocabulary and structures.

In the US This feature is a short cultural reading or brief explanation of some aspect of US culture.

Compare Cultures At levels 1–4, this follow-up to In the US asks learners to compare the custom or situation in the US to similar ones in their home countries.

Activities A, B, C, etc. These practice activities, most of them interactive, apply what has been learned in the lesson so far.

Lesson Tasks Each lesson concludes with a task that encourages learners to apply the skills taught and practiced earlier. Many tasks involve pair or group work, as well as follow-up presentations to the class.

Challenge Reading

At level 4, a two-page reading follows the lessons. This feature helps learners develop skills that prepare them for longer readings they will encounter in future study or higher-level jobs.

Unit Project

Each unit concludes with a final project in which learners apply all or many of the skills they acquired in the unit. The project consists of carefully structured and sequenced individual, pair, and group activities. These projects also help develop important higher-level skills such as planning, organizing, collaborating, and presenting.

Additional Features

The following minifeatures appear as needed at different levels:

One Step Up These extensions of an activity, task, or unit project allow learners to work at a slightly higher skill level. This feature is especially useful when classes include learners at multiple levels.

Attention Boxes These unlabeled boxes highlight words and structures that are not taught explicitly in the lesson, but that learners may need. Teachers are encouraged to point out these words and structures and to offer any explanations that learners require.

Remember? These boxes present, in abbreviated form, previously introduced vocabulary and language structures.

Writing Extension This feature encourages learners to do additional writing. It is usually a practical rather than an academic activity.

Technology Extra This extension gives learners guidelines for doing part of an activity, task, or project using such technology as computers, photocopiers, and audio and video recorders.

Contents

Unit 5   What's for Dinner?

◆ Vocabulary: Foods • Coupons
◆ Language: Count and noncount nouns • *There is* and *there are*
  • Questions and answers with *or*
◆ Pronunciation: Intonation with words in a list
◆ Culture: Fast food

Unit 6   Call the Police!

◆ Vocabulary: Home inventory words • Police report words • Describing people
◆ Language: Past-tense statements with *be* • Past-tense statements with regular and irregular verbs • Past-tense questions with *be* and other verbs
◆ Pronunciation: Long and short *i* sounds • Past-tense ending sounds
◆ Culture: Neighborhood Watch programs in the US

Unit 7   Succeeding at School

◆ Vocabulary: School words • Report cards • After-school activities
◆ Language: Possessive adjectives • Compound sentences with *and* • Future tense with *going to*
◆ Pronunciation: Long and short *o* sounds
◆ Culture: Parent participation in schools

Unit 8   I Want a Good Job!

◆ Vocabulary: Employment words • Educational opportunities
◆ Language: *Can* and *can't* • Compound sentences with *but* • *A, an, the*
◆ Pronunciation: Long and short *u* sounds
◆ Culture: Education can increase income

Are You Ready?

Starting in English

Home 1   Work/School 2   Community 3

◆ **Vocabulary** Information • Days and Months • Weather • Time • Transportation • Classroom directions • School supplies • Money

◆ **Language** Subject pronouns with *be* • Contractions with *be* • Possessive nouns and adjectives • *Need, need to* • Plurals of regular nouns

◆ **Pronunciation** Syllable stress

◆ **Culture** Class rules in the US

Where is your information?

Tomas is at the school.
The clerk needs information.

Think and Talk

1. What do you see?
2. What's the problem?
3. Do you have your information?

= number
clerk
information
problem
ready
registration

Picture Dictionary   Listen. Repeat. Circle new words. Write the words.

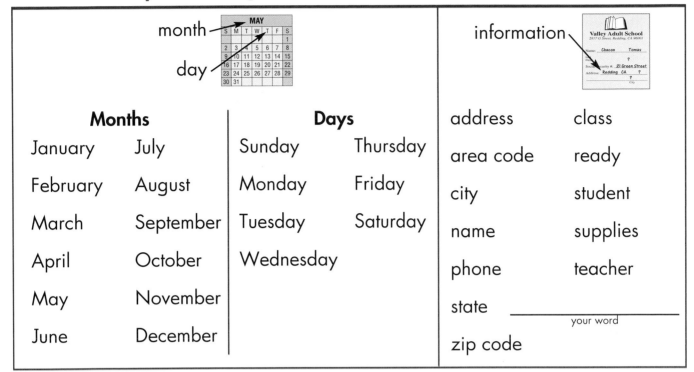

month
day

information

Months		**Days**	
January	July	Sunday	Thursday
February	August	Monday	Friday
March	September	Tuesday	Saturday
April	October	Wednesday	
May	November		
June	December		

address   class

area code   ready

city   student

name   supplies

phone   teacher

state   _____

zip code   your word

Gather Your Thoughts   Make a chart like this one.

Write your information.

Your School Information	
Name: Adeuito R. Lopes	**Phone:** 5083863414
Address: 86 Winthrop St	
School:	**Class Days/Times:**
Address:	

What's the Problem?   Are you ready for school? Why?

Why not? Think or talk with a partner.

Setting Goals   Check ✔ your goals.

❑ 1. Tell the month and day.
❑ 2. Talk about the weather.
❑ 3. Talk about transportation.

❑ 4. Follow classroom directions.
❑ 5. Talk about school supplies.
❑ 6. Be ready for school.

I'm Lost! I'm Late!

◆ Talk about the time and weather

◆ Talk about transportation

◆ Use *be*, subject pronouns, and contractions

glasses
late
lost
need
rainy

Are you at school on time?

◆ **Reading Tip** A picture tells many things. What do the pictures tell you about Tomas?

Idiom Watch!
get up
on time

Today is the first day of school. Tomas is late.

Tomas is in his car. It's rainy. He's lost.

Speak or Circle

1. Today is the first day of school. (Yes) No

2. Tomas gets up at 7:30 A.M. Yes No

3. It is a rainy day. Yes No

4. Tomas is on time for school. Yes No

Picture Dictionary   Listen. Repeat. Circle new words. Write the words.

Weather   How's the weather?

It's cloudy.

It's rainy.

It's sunny.

Time   The class starts at 8:30.

early

late

on time

Transportation

drive a car   ride a bike   take a bus   take a train   walk

Class Chat   Walk around. Ask questions.
Write answers in your chart.

How do you go to school?   I walk.

What is your name?	How do you go to school?
I'm Toni.	I walk.

Grammar Talk: Subject Pronouns with *Be*

Subject Pronoun	Verb *Be*	(Contraction)		Subject Pronoun	Verb *Be*	(Contraction)	
I	am	(I'm)	a student.	He	is	(He's)	a teacher.
You	are	(You're)	Tomas.	She	is	(She's)	lost.
We	are	(We're)	students.	It	is	(It's)	sunny.
They	are	(They're)	late.				

What letters are missing in the contractions? Write the letters with your teacher.

Activity A   Use the words in the sentences.

rainy	It	late	✔ is

1. It _____is_____ Monday.

2. It is ___rainy___ .

3. ___it is___ is 9:00.

4. Raul is ___late___ for school.

Monday 9:00

Activity B   Use the words in the sentences.

✔ It	early	It's	sunny

1. _____It_____ is Friday.

2. It is ___sunny___ .

3. ___it is___ 8:20.

4. Raul is ___early___ for school.

Friday 8:20

Activity C   Draw a picture of you going to school.
Write about today.

_____

_____

_____

_____

TASK 1 Make a Class List

How do students go to school? Do they take the bus?
Do they walk? Ask students. Make a list.

list = 1. _____
2. _____
3. _____

14 *Warm-Up Unit Lesson 1*

Work/School

Welcome!

◆ Follow classroom directions

◆ Use possessive nouns and adjectives

What does your teacher say in class?

◆ **Listening Tip** 🎧 Listen for the words that you know. Circle the words. Write the words. You can read the words on page 118.

| answer |
| book |
| bring |
| do |
| open |
| pencil |
| write |

The teacher talks to the class.

Speak or Circle

1. Tomas is on time to class.   Yes   (No)

2. Tomas is from Chile.   (Yes)   No

3. Tomas needs a pencil.   (Yes)   No

4. The teacher is Mr. Pat.   Yes   (No)

Picture Dictionary   Listen. Repeat. Circle new words. Write the words.

answer

aberto open

Falar talk

ask

braço levantado raise (your hand)

ver tell

listen

Soletrar spell

escrever write

Class Chat   Walk around. Give directions to students in the class.

Tell me your name.	Spell it.
Maria Sanchez	M-a-r-i-a S-a-n-c-h-e-z

Tell me your name.

Maria Sanchez

Grammar Talk: Possessive Nouns and Adjectives

Tomas	Tomas's	Tomas's phone number is 916-555-1928.
Maria	Maria's	Maria's address is 5876 Hillside Road.
the teacher	the teacher's	The teacher's name is Mr. Allen.

What changes in the words Tomas, Maria, *and* teacher?

I	**my**	Check **my** answers.	we	**our**	Check **our** numbers.
you	**your**	Spell **your** name.	you	**your**	Write **your** answers.
he	**his**	Answer **his** question.	they	**their**	Read **their** words.
she	**her**	Read **her** answer.			

Pronunciation Target • Syllable Stress

🎧 *Listen to the teacher or the audio.*

late   *student*   *directions*

16   *Warm-Up Unit Lesson 2*

Activity A   Look at the ID cards. Write.

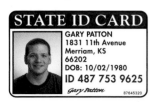

One Step Up
Tell your partner your information. Begin with "My . . . ." Use these words.

first name	last name
address	city
state	zip code
phone number	area code

1. _____Gary's_____ address is 1831 11th Avenue.

   His address is 1831 11th Avenue.

2. _____His_____ birthday is October 2.   *2?*

   _____

3. _____Her_____ last name is Martinez.

   _____

4. _____ zip code is 02139.

   _____

In the US   Class Rules

Be on time.
Raise your hand to talk.
Call your teacher by name.
Say "Mr. Allen" or "Ms. Bay," not "Teacher."

☞ **Compare Cultures**

What is the same in classes in your country? Make a list.

same

TASK 2   Make a Name Card

- Write your first name and last name on Side A.
- Write your address, home country, and language on Side B.
- Put your name card on your desk.

Money for School!

◆ Count money
◆ Use plurals
◆ Use *need, need to*

What do you need for school?

◆ **Reading Tip** Read the sign. Read the sentences in Speak or Circle. Find words from the sign in the sentences.

Where's my money?

(handwritten note)
found encontra
find
hide
need Preciso
need to
pay
sale
sandwich
sign
store

Money for School

Tomas needs money for school.

The bus is $1.25. A sandwich is $3.00.

He is at the store.

He needs a notebook and 5 pencils.

He needs to pay. He needs to find his money.

Speak or Circle

1. Tomas needs work supplies.   Yes   (No)
2. A notebook is $5.00.   Yes   (No)
3. A pen is $2.00.   (Yes)   No
4. A dictionary is $4.95.   Yes   (No)

Learn

Picture Dictionary   Listen. Repeat. Circle new words. Write the words.

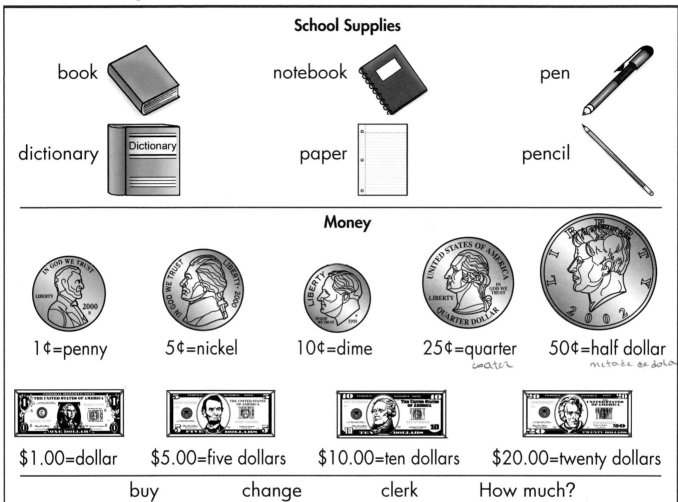

School Supplies

book

notebook

pen

dictionary

paper

pencil

Money

1¢=penny

5¢=nickel

10¢=dime

25¢=quarter

coater

50¢=half dollar

mitate de dola

$1.00=dollar

$5.00=five dollars

$10.00=ten dollars

$20.00=twenty dollars

buy   change   clerk   How much?

Class Chat   Walk around. Ask questions.
Write answers in your chart.

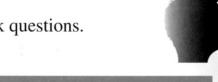

What's your name?	What do you need for school?
Nina	paper and a dictionary

What do you need for school?

I need paper and a dictionary.

Grammar Talk: Plurals of Regular Nouns		Using *Need* and *Need To*
I need a **book.**	I need two **books.**	I **need** $3.00.
The **pen** is blue.	The **pens** are blue.	I **need to** pay $3.00.
Most nouns add s *for plurals:* book ⟶ books		*What kind of word follows* need? *What follows* need to? *Talk to your teacher.*

Activity A 🎧 Listen to your teacher or the audio. Write the numbers.

1. How much are two notebooks?   Two notebooks are __6__.

2. How much are four pens?   Four pens are __8__.

3. How much are 10 pencils?   Ten pencils are _____.

4. How much is the paper?   The paper is _____.

Check your answers with your partner. Read the questions and answers with your partner.

One Step Up
Partner A reads the question from Activity A. Partner B reads the answer. Use a pronoun.
A: How much are two notebooks?
B: They are $6.00.

Remember?

$ dollar

¢ cents

$2.00 = two dollars

$3.95 = three ninety-five

Activity B 🎧 Tomas is at the store. He talks to a clerk.
Listen to Tomas and the clerk. Put the conversation in order.

__7__ OK. Here's $10.00.

__3__ I need a notebook and a dictionary.

__1__ I need to buy school supplies.

__5__ Spanish-English, please.

__8__ And $1.55 in change.

__4__ English or Spanish-English?

__2__ What supplies do you need?

__6__ That's $8.45.

Read the conversation with your partner. Check your work.

TASK 3 Get Ready to Buy School Supplies

Think about supplies you need for school. What do you have? What do you need? Make a list. Talk to your partner. How are your lists the same? How are they different?

different = not the same

Make a New Student Booklet

Do these things to plan a New Student Booklet.

Get Ready

Work in four groups.

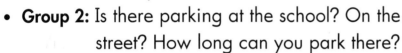

- **Group 1:** Find the information about the school. What is the name of the school, the address, phone number, teacher's name, room number? What are the days and hours of the class? What are the school holidays?
- **Group 2:** Is there parking at the school? On the street? How long can you park there?
- **Group 3:** What does a new student need to know in class? Write classroom directions. Use pictures and words.
- **Group 4:** List supplies. What do new students need? Where can students get the supplies? List stores and addresses.

holiday
parking
store

Do the Work

Use the paper from your teacher.

- **Group 1:** Write the name, address, phone number, and other information about your school.
- **Group 2:** Write the places to park at the school. Write the streets where you can park.
- **Group 3:** Write classroom directions for new students.
- **Group 4:** List the supplies that students need to buy.

Present Your Project

Talk to the class about your information. Make copies of the New Student Booklet.

📟💻 Technology Extra
Make a cover for your booklet on the computer.

My Life Is Changing!

Helping Your Family

Home
1

Community
2

Work/School
3

◆ **Vocabulary** Relatives • Neighborhood places • Job ads

◆ **Language** Negative contractions with *be* • *Yes/no* questions and answers with *be* • Commands • Prepositions of location

◆ **Pronunciation** Question and answer intonation

◆ **Culture** Job interviews in the US

Where are your relatives?

Nassim reads a letter from her parents.

change
help
letter
relative
parents = mother and father
want

Think and Talk

1. What do you see?
2. What's the problem?
3. Who lives with you?
4. Do you help your parents?
   ❑ a lot   ❑ some   ❑ a little   ❑ not at all

Picture Dictionary   Listen. Repeat. Circle new words. Write the words.

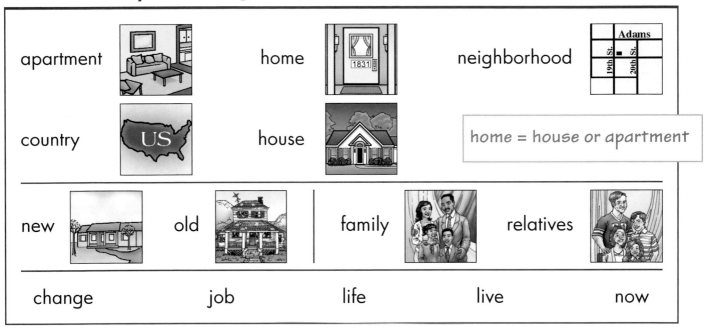

apartment

home

neighborhood

country

house

home = house or apartment

new

old

family

relatives

change   job   life   live   now

Gather Your Thoughts   Complete the chart for you.

My Life Is Changing		
	In My Home Country	**In the US**
My Name		
My Job		
House or Apartment?		
People in My Home		

home country = the country you are from

What's the Problem?   Think about your life. What do you want to change now? What do you want to change later? Use the words in the Picture Dictionary. Think or talk with a partner.

later

Setting Goals   Check ✔ your goals.

❏ **1.** Talk about my family.

❏ **2.** Find places in my neighborhood.

❏ **3.** Complete a job application.

❏ **4.** Another goal: _____

Home

A Family Problem

◆ Talk about family members
◆ Use subject pronouns and negative contractions with *be*

Do you help your relatives? How?

◆ **Reading Tip**   Read the story. Read the questions. Read the story again. Find answers.

housewife
married
small
well

Nassim's Story

Nassim is married to a nurse.

Nassim is a housewife with two daughters.

She and her family live in California.

They live in a small apartment.

Nassim's parents live in New York.

They aren't well.

They are old.

They need help.

They want to live with Nassim.

Speak or Circle

1. Nassim is a nurse.   True   False

2. Nassim's daughters need help.   True   False

3. There are changes in Nassim's life.   True   False

Picture Dictionary Listen. Repeat. Circle new words. Write the words.

grandfather + grandmother = grandparents

father + mother = parents

daughter + son = children

husband   wife

brother   sister

_____   _____
       your word   your word

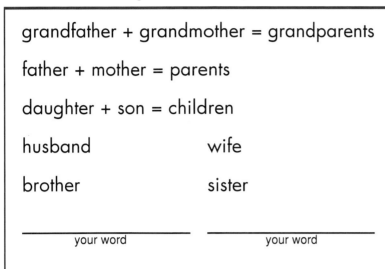

Family Tree

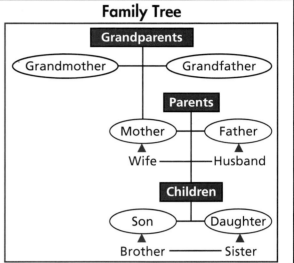

Class Chat Walk around. Ask questions.
Write answers in your chart.

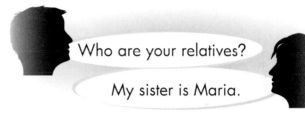

Who are your relatives?

My sister is Maria.

What's your name?	Where are you from?	Who are your relatives?	Where is she or he?
Teresa	Ecuador	My sister is Maria.	She's in New York.

Grammar Talk: Negative Contractions with *Be*

I am not	I'm not		his brother.
You are not	You're not	You aren't	his sister.
He is not	He's not	He isn't	from the US.
She is not	She's not	She isn't	from Kenya.
It is not	It's not	It isn't	from Mexico.
We are not	We're not	We aren't	in New York.
You are not	You're not	You aren't	brothers.
They are not	They're not	They aren't	sisters.

*What are the missing letters in the contractions? Talk about this
question with your teacher.*

Activity A Ask and answer the questions with a partner.

| Kip | Paka | Lusala | Nassim | Jamie | Samantha |

1.	Is Jamie Nassim's mother?		Yes	No
2.	Are Nassim and Lusala Samantha's parents?		Yes	No
3.	Is Paka Nassim's daughter?		Yes	No
4.	Are Kip and Paka Samantha's grandparents?		Yes	No
5.	Is Kip Paka's husband?		Yes	No

Activity B Look at the chart. Tell your group what you are. Put an *X* in the box.

My name is David. I am a father and a son.

Name	Grand-mother	Grand-father	Mother	Father	Brother	Sister	Son	Daughter
David				X			X	

 TASK 1 Draw Your Family Tree

Write names on your family tree. Talk to a partner about your family.

Helen isn't my mother. She isn't my grandmother. She's my sister.

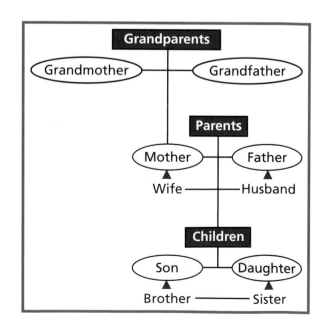

 Writing Extension Write the names of three of your relatives. Write two sentences about each one.

Nacho isn't my father. He's my brother.

The Neighborhood

◆ Find places in your neighborhood
◆ Use yes/no questions and answers

Are you worried about your family?

bedroom
expensive
maybe
opinion
part-time
problem
worried

◆ **Listening Tip** 🎧 Listen for the words that you know. Write the words. You can read the words on page 118.

Speak or Circle

1. Is Nassim worried?   Yes   No
2. Is the apartment big?   Yes   No
3. Does Nassim need a part-time job?   Yes   No

What's Your Opinion?   Is this a good time for Nassim to get a job?

❏ Yes   ❏ Maybe   ❏ No

Picture Dictionary   Listen. Repeat. Circle new words. Write the words.

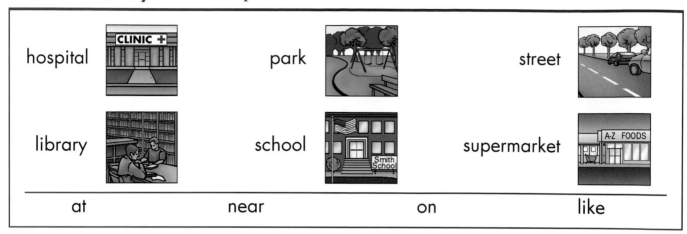

| hospital | | park | | street | |
| library | | school | | supermarket | |

| at | near | on | like |

| Where do you live? | I live **on River Street**. |
| What's your address? | I live **at 1114** River Street. |

Partner Chat   Walk around. Ask questions. Write answers in your chart.

Where do you live?

I live on River Street.

What's your name?	Where do you live?	What's your address?	What's it near?
Carmen	I live on Front Street.	I live at 4113 Front Street.	It's near a park.

Grammar Talk: Yes/No Questions and Answers with _Be_

	Question with _Be_	Short Answer
Nassim is in her apartment.	**Is Nassim** in her apartment?	Yes, she **is**.
Jamie and Samantha are at school.	**Are they** at the park?	No, they **aren't**.

Where is the verb be _in questions? Where is_ be _in short answers?_

Pronunciation Target • Question and Answer Intonation

🎧 _Listen to your teacher or the audio._

Is Nassim at home? ↗   Yes, she is. ↘

Activity A   Talk to a partner. Ask three yes/no
questions about the people in your partner's family.

Is your daughter
at school?

Yes, she is.

Activity B   With a partner, complete the conversation.
Use these words.

✔apartment   expensive   near   neighborhood   park   school

Apartment for rent.
3 bedrooms.
Near the park.
3746 Bay Street
555-2720

Oak Park

Bay Street

X

expensive = $$$
I don't know.

Lusala: Look! An _____apartment_____ with three
                bedrooms.
                        1

Nassim: I like this _____. The apartment is
                        2

                near the _____. And it's near our
                        3

                daughters' _____.
                        4

Lusala: It's also _____ the hospital where
                        5

                I work. It's in a good place.

Nassim: Is it _____?
                        6

Lusala: I don't know. We need to call.

One Step Up
Write the sentences in your
notebook. Answer the
questions.

1. Is a house for rent?
2. Is an apartment for rent?
3. Is the apartment near a
   park?

Read the conversation with your partner.

TASK 2   Draw a Map
In your group, draw a map of the street where your school is.
Write the name of the street. Write names of other buildings.

building
map

Jobs, Jobs, Jobs!

◆ Complete a job application
◆ Use commands

ad
aide
apply
experience
hotel
in person
necessary
required
restaurant
server
8–12 = 8 to 12
M–F = Monday to Friday

What job is good for you?

◆ **Reading Tip**   Read the ads. Read the questions. Look for the same words in the ads and the questions.

resume to: 555-8675

Restaurant Servers; Hours 5-10 PM, Tues.-Sat. nights. Apply in person on Mondays 1-5 p.m.

Central Hotel Secretary; Computer experience; 1352 Main Street; Full-time. Apply online www.centralhotel.com

skills needed. Call 555-2345.

River City School Teacher's Aide; No experience necessary. 8-12 noon M-F; English required. Call 555-2876.

Nurses RN's LPN's CNA's needed. Apply now to Central Medical. Send

Apply online = Apply on the Internet

Speak or Circle

1. Is there a full-time job at Central Hotel?   Yes   No

2. Do you need English for the school job?   Yes   No

3. Is the restaurant job from 1 to 5 P.M.?   Yes   No

What's Your Opinion?   The restaurant job is good for Nassim.

❏ Yes   ❏ Maybe   ❏ No

Class Chat
Walk around. Ask questions. Write answers in your chart.

What's your job?

I'm a server.

What's your name?	What's your job?	How do you learn about jobs?
Natalia	I'm a server.	From friends.

Grammar Talk: Commands

Sign your name.	**Circle** the letter.
Call 555-4242.	**Spell** your last name.
Print your information.	**Tell** me your phone number.

Commands tell you to do something. Use the base form of verbs in commands.

Base forms = be, need, want, live, sign, call, do

Activity A
Class Chat Follow-Up Look at your Class Chat chart. Write sentences in your notebook.

Natalia is a server. She learns about jobs from friends.

In the US   Job Interviews

		In the US	In My Country
🕐	Be on time.		
🤝	Shake hands.		
😊	Smile.		
👞	Wear nice clothes.		
🗣	Tell good things about you.		

Vocabulary
Listen. Repeat. Circle and write new words.

ad

application

education

experience

interview

call

circle

print

sign

full-time

part-time

_____

your word

Remember?

spell   tell

☛ **Compare Cultures**

Are these five things the same in your home country? Write **yes** or **no**.

Activity B   Read Nassim's application. Write commands in the sentences.

RIVER CITY SCHOOL APPLICATION FOR EMPLOYMENT				Print your information.

Name: Mr. (Mrs.) Ms.	Keino	Nassim	999-33-2222
Circle one	Last	First	SS#

1114 Ridge Street	Sacramento	CA	95818	(916) 555-1234
Address	City	State	Zip	Phone

EDUCATION

Dates			School
From: 1976	*To:* 1980	Nairobi High School
From: 1980	*To:* 1984	Moi University
From: 2001	*To:* 2003	Sacramento Adult School
From:	*To:*	

WORK EXPERIENCE   List your last job first.

Dates	*From:* 1988 *To:* 1989
Job	English Teacher
Employer	Nairobi High School

Sign your name.

1. _____Print_____ your information.

2. _____ one: Mr. Mrs. Ms.

3. _____ your name.

4. _____ your last job first.

One Step Up

In your notebook, write five yes/no questions about the application.

Is 95817 Nassim's zip code?

 TASK 3 Information, Please!

Interview your partner. Write your partner's information on the application.
Say "Tell me" to get information.
Say "Spell it" to write a new word.

Tell me your name, please.

Nassim Keino.

Spell it, please.

N-A-S-S-I-M
K-E-I-N-O

APPLICATION FOR EMPLOYMENT				Print your information.

Name: Mr. Mrs. Ms.			
Circle one	Last	First	SS#

Address	City	State	Zip	Phone

Writing Personal Information

Plan, write, and present your Personal Information Sheet.

Get Ready

What do you need? Driver's license? Passport? Social Security card? Find your information.

Do the Work

Complete the Personal Information Sheet from your teacher. Check your work. Is it correct?

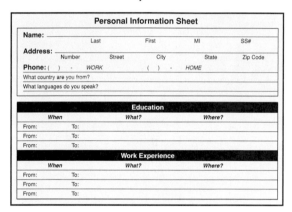

business
keep

Present Your Project

Talk to your group or the class about your Personal Information Sheet.

- Where do you live?
- What country are you from?
- What work experience do you have?

One Step Up

Go to a business. Ask for an application. Complete the application. Use your Personal Information Sheet. Give the application to your teacher to check your work.

Writing Extension Use your Personal Information Sheet. Write five sentences.

My name is Julia Gutierrez. I live at 1036 East Street. I live in Washington. I am from Mexico. I speak Spanish and English.

Technology Extra
Photocopy your Personal Information Sheet. Keep one copy with you.
Keep one copy at home.

I Need to Plan a Party

Planning an Activity

Work/School   Community   Home
      1   2   3

◆ **Vocabulary** Party plans • Work schedules

◆ **Language** Present-tense verbs • Prepositions of time
   • Frequency adverbs • Present-tense *yes/no* questions
   and answers

◆ **Pronunciation** Present-tense ending sounds • Long and short
   a sounds

◆ **Culture** Birthday parties in the US

Are birthday parties important?

Pavel wants a birthday party. His mother needs help. His father works on Saturdays.

Think and Talk

1. What do you see?

2. What's the problem?

3. When do you have parties?

What's Your Opinion? Do Pavel's mother and father need to invite all his friends?

❑ Yes   ❑ Maybe   ❑ No

Picture Dictionary Listen. Repeat. Circle new words. Write the words.

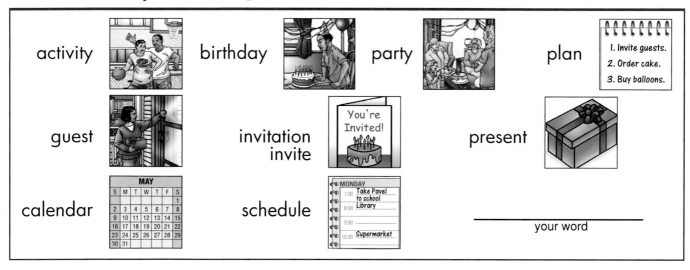

activity   birthday   party   plan
1. Invite guests.
2. Order cake.
3. Buy balloons.

guest   invitation
invite   present

calendar   schedule   _____
your word

Gather Your Thoughts   Who do you have parties for?

Make an idea map in your notebook. Here's an example.

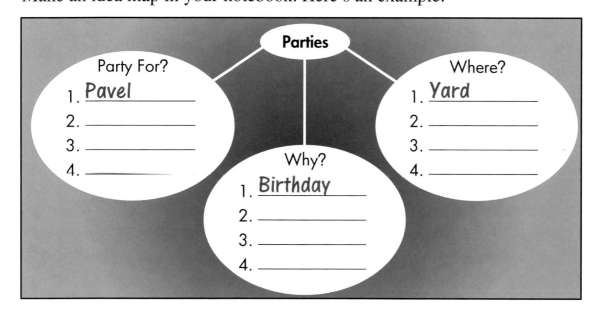

Parties

Party For?
1. Pavel
2. _____
3. _____
4. _____

Why?
1. Birthday
2. _____
3. _____
4. _____

Where?
1. Yard
2. _____
3. _____
4. _____

What's the Problem?   Are birthday parties expensive?

Do they take a lot of time to plan? Think or talk with a partner.

Setting Goals   Check ✔ your goals.

❑ **1.** Write a note.
❑ **2.** Change a work schedule.
❑ **3.** Invite people to an activity.
❑ **4.** Plan an activity.
❑ **5.** Plan for changes.
❑ **6.** Another goal: _____

I Need a Favor!

◆ Read a schedule
◆ Write a note
◆ Use present-tense verbs and prepositions of time

| bakery |
| favor |
| trade |

What's your work or school schedule?

◆ **Reading Tip** To read a chart, look at the words on the left side and the words at the top. In the schedule for Pat's Bakery, what words are on the left side? What words are on the top?

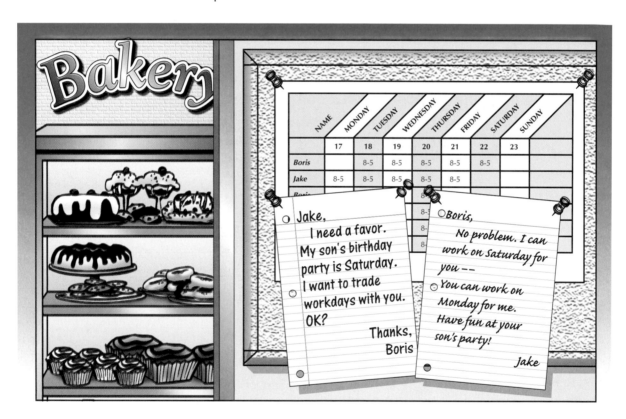

Speak or Circle

1. Boris works on Monday, Tuesday, and Wednesday.   True   (False)

2. Jake and Boris work five days a week.   True   False

3. Boris writes Jake a note.   True   False

4. Jake asks Boris for a favor.   True   False

5. Jake says it's OK to trade days.   True   False

Partner Chat   Talk to a partner. Ask questions. Write answers in your chart.

What time do you start work or school?

I start at 8 A.M.

Vocabulary

Listen. Repeat. Circle and write new words.

favor

note

trade

work

end

go

start

A.M.

P.M.

What's your name?	What time do you start work or school?	What time do you end work or school?
Jolie	8:00 a.m.	5:00 p.m.

Grammar Talk: Present-Tense Verbs

Subject	Verb		Subject	do + not	(Contraction)	Verb
I	need	help.	I	do not	(don't)	need help.
You	work	today.	You	do not	(don't)	work today.
We	trade	days.	We	do not	(don't)	trade days.
They	write	notes.	They	do not	(don't)	write notes.
He	wants	a party.	He	does not	(doesn't)	want a party.
She	works	at home.	She	does not	(doesn't)	work at home.
It	ends	at 5:00.	It	does not	(doesn't)	end at 5:00.

Some verbs have different forms.

I **have** (don't have) to work.   She **has** (doesn't have) to work.

I **go** (don't go) to school on Friday. He **goes** (doesn't go) to school on Friday.

What words make a verb negative? Talk with your teacher.

Pronunciation Target • Present-Tense Endings

🎧 *Listen to your teacher or the audio.*

wants   likes   writes   needs   agrees   ends

Activity A   Talk to your partner. Ask the questions.
Circle *Yes* or *No*. Write about your partner.

One Step Up
Write complete sentences.
She doesn't like her
work schedule.

Do you like your work
or school schedule?

No, I don't.

1. Do you like your work schedule?   Yes   (No)
2. Do you need a job?   Yes   No
3. Do you want a different job?   Yes   No

The birthday party is <u>on</u> Saturday.
It is <u>at</u> 1:00 P.M.   = starts at 1:00 P.M.
It is <u>from</u> 1:00 P.M. <u>to</u> 3:00 P.M. = starts at 1:00 P.M. and ends at 3:00 P.M.

Activity B   Talk to your group. Ask
questions. Write answers in sentences.

Who gets up at
6 A.M.?

I get up at
6 A.M.

1. Who gets up at 6 A.M.? _____

2. Who lives near a school? _____

3. Who works five days a week? _____

4. Who doesn't speak Spanish? _____

5. Who likes birthday parties? _____

TASK 1   Trade a Favor

You need a favor. You need help to buy a present or to talk to
your teacher or to plan a party. Write a note to your partner.
What do you need? Write four sentences. Read Boris's note
to Jake on page 36 for an example.

One Step Up
Read your note to your class.
Find someone to trade favors
with.

Planning the Party

◆ Talk about asking for advice
◆ Use frequency adverbs

Who gives you advice?

◆ **Reading Tip**   Read the story. Write new words in a notebook.

advice
feel
neighbor
nervous
of course
yard

> Rosa, I need some help.

> Of course, Yelena. We like to plan parties.

Pavel's Birthday

Yelena feels nervous about the party. Who can help her?

She asks her neighbors, Rosa and Jack, for advice. They help Yelena make plans.

First, they make a list of what they need—a place, a guest list, supplies, and food.

Jack thinks the yard is a good place. Pavel tells Yelena the names of his friends.

Rosa tells Yelena where to buy invitations and balloons.

Now they need a cake.

Of course! Boris makes beautiful birthday cakes!

Speak or Circle

1. Yelena feels nervous about the   a. neighbors   b. advice   c. party
2. Yelena asks her neighbors for   a. plans   b. advice   c. presents
3. Jack wants the party in the   a. yard   b. school   c. home

Group Chat   Walk around. Ask questions. Write answers in a chart.

Who helps you plan activities?

My sister, Olga.

Use your chart. Write sentences in your notebook.

Susan plans meetings at church. Her friends help.

In the US   Birthday Parties

People in the US sometimes send invitations for parties.
Invitations tell the date, time, and place of the party.
It is polite to be on time.
People often buy presents for birthday parties.

☞ Compare Cultures

Talk to your group. How do you celebrate birthdays in your
home country? Do you have parties? Do you have birthday
cakes? Do you buy presents? Fill out the chart.

0%	25%	50%	75%	100%
Never	Rarely	Sometimes	Often	Always

Vocabulary

Listen. Repeat. Circle and write new words.

balloons

cake

celebrate

friend

happy

help

list

make

date

meeting

place

send

always

never

often

rarely

sometimes

Name _____		Home Country _____		
	Always	**Often**	**Sometimes**	**Rarely**	**Never**
Parties					
Cakes					
Presents					

Activity A   Write the correct words in the sentence.

at	buy	✔ from	makes	at	sends	on	✔ plan

1. Yelena and Rosa _____plan_____ the party _____from_____
   1:00 P.M. to 3:00 P.M.

2. Pavel _____ invitations _____ Monday.

3. On Saturday they _____ balloons _____ 9:00 A.M.

4. Boris _____ the birthday cake _____ 11 A.M.

Read the sentences to your partner.

Activity B   Look at a calendar. Ask people in your class questions. Write in your notebook.

What's your name?	What day is your birthday this year?	What do you want?
Lisa	Tuesday	clothes

One Step Up
With your class, count the birthdays on Monday, Tuesday, and other days. Make a class chart that shows how many birthdays are on each day.

TASK 2   Who Gives You Advice?

In your group, think about an activity you need to plan for your home, school, work, or community. Do you need help? Who can give you advice?

	Name	Activity	What do I need help with?	Who can give me advice?
Work	Josef	Meeting	Bring coffee	Friend at work
School				
Home				
Community				

Changing Plans!

◆ Change plans
◆ Use present tense with *yes/no* questions and answers

porch
run
take

Why do you change plans?

◆ **Listening Tip** 🎧 Listen to people talk. Think about how they feel. Are they happy, sad, worried? Listen to your teacher or the audio. What happens at the party? Is Yelena worried? Are the children happy or sad? You can read the words on page 118.

Speak or Circle

1. How is the weather?   a. sunny   b. windy   c. rainy
2. Where do they go?   a. home   b. the park   c. the porch
3. Who takes the presents?   a. Pavel   b. Yelena   c. Boris
4. Who has the cake?   a. Pavel   b. Yelena   c. Boris

Class Chat Walk around. Ask questions. Write answers in your chart.

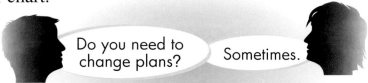

Do you need to change plans?

Sometimes.

Name	Do you need to change plans?	Why?
Selma	Sometimes	My work schedule changes.

Activity A **Class Chat Follow-Up** Look at the Class Chat information. Write four questions beginning with *Do* or *Does*. Exchange papers with a partner. Write the answers to your partner's questions.

Does Selma need to change plans? Yes, sometimes.

Grammar Talk: Present-Tense Yes/No Questions and Answers

Question		Yes Answer	No Answer	(Contractions)
Do	I need to call?	Yes, you **do.**	No, you **do not**	(don't).
Do	we like parties?	Yes, we **do.**	No, we **do not**	(don't).
Do	they see balloons?	Yes, they **do.**	No, they **do not**	(don't).
Does	he like his presents?	Yes, he **does.**	No, he **does not**	(doesn't).
Does	she eat some cake?	Yes, she **does.**	No, she **does not**	(doesn't).
Does	it rain at the party?	Yes, it **does.**	No, it **does not**	(doesn't).

What is the first word in the question? What is the last word in the Yes *answer? What is the last word in the* No *answer? Talk to your teacher about these questions.*

Pronunciation Target • Long and Short *a* Sounds

🎧 *Listen to your teacher or the audio.*

rain   cake   favor   plan   at   glad

Activity B 🎧 Listen to your teacher or the audio. Write numbers 1 to 7 to put the conversation in the correct order.

_____ **Pavel:** Thanks for the backpack, Ben. It's great!

_____ **Ben:** I'm glad you like it. Thanks for the cake. Mom, Pavel's dad makes great cakes.

_____ **Miguel:** Hi, Boris. Thank you for inviting Ben to the party.

__1__ **Miguel:** Hello, Yelena. I am Miguel and this is Sylvia. We are Ben's parents.

_____ **Yelena:** It's nice to meet you, Miguel and Sylvia. This is my husband, Boris.

_____ **Boris:** It's nice to have Ben here. Pavel, thank Ben for his present.

_____ **Sylvia:** Really? I need to call you, Boris. I need a cake for a church meeting next week.

backpack

Really? = True?

One Step Up
Write the conversation in the correct order.

Activity C Read the questions to your partner. Write yes/no answers.

1. Do Ben's parents meet Boris and Yelena? __Yes, they do.__

2. Does Miguel thank Pavel for inviting Ben? _____

3. Does Pavel thank Sylvia for his present? _____

4. Does Ben like the cake? _____

TASK 3 Talk About Changing Plans

You and your partner plan a party for your class. Think about the day of the party:

• Someone forgets the food. What can you do?

• Your party is outside. It rains. What can you do? Where do you go?

• Think about two other problems. What can you do?

Plan a Party!

Do these things to plan, prepare, and have a party.

Get Ready

- What kind of party do you want? A birthday party? A holiday party? Or?
- Make a list of people to invite (teachers, students, friends, relatives).
- What time is the party? How long is it?
- What do you need? Food? Music?
- Do you need advice? Who do you ask?

Make a chart with this information.

Invitations to
1.
2.
3.
4.
5.

We Need
Food—Olga, Ramon, Sara
Music—Mei and Esteban

Do the Work

- Make invitations with the date, time, and place.
- Send the invitations.

Please Come to Our Party

Date: Friday, December 20
Time: 2:00 to 4:00 p.m
Place: Central Adult School
2543 Main Street, Room 202

Present Your Project

Have your party! At the party:

- Welcome your guests.
- Thank them for coming.
- Have a good time!

 **Technology Extra**

Make your invitation on the computer. Make copies on the copy machine.

How Do You Feel?

Getting Medical Help

Work/School
1

Community
2

Home
3

◆ **Vocabulary** Common illnesses and symptoms • Question words • Medicine labels

◆ **Language** Object pronouns • Present-tense *Wh-* questions with *be* • Present-tense *Wh-* questions with other verbs

◆ **Pronunciation** Intonation with *be* and *Wh-* questions

◆ **Culture** Home remedies in the US

stay home

How do you feel today?

Today is Monday.
Jim doesn't feel well.
He has a big meeting at work.

Think and Talk

1. What do you see?
2. What's the problem?
3. When do you stay home from work or school?

What's Your Opinion? Do sick people need to stay home?

❑ always ❑ sometimes ❑ never

Picture Dictionary   Listen. Repeat. Circle new words. Write the words.

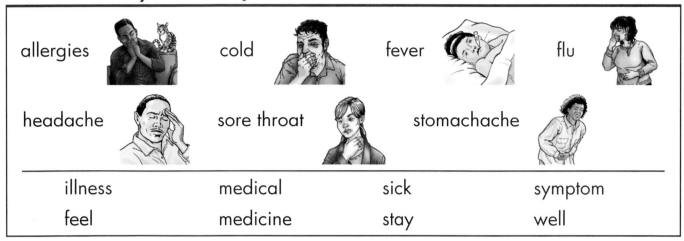

allergies   cold   fever   flu

headache   sore throat   stomachache

| illness | medical | sick | symptom |
| feel | medicine | stay | well |

Gather Your Thoughts   What do you do when you're sick?

Make an idea map. Write what you do. Here's an example.

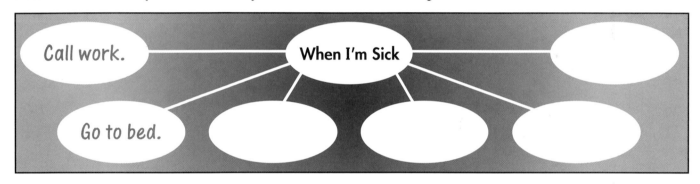

Call work.   When I'm Sick

Go to bed.

What's the Problem?   Is it easy to get good medical help in the US? Think or talk with a partner.

Setting Goals   Check ✔ your healthcare goals.

❏ **1.** Make a doctor's appointment.
❏ **2.** Call in sick to work or school.
❏ **3.** Complete a medical information form.
❏ **4.** Read a medicine label.
❏ **5.** Ask questions with *who, what, when, where, why.*
❏ **6.** Talk about illnesses and symptoms.
❏ **7.** Another goal: _____

Sick at Work

◆ Ask for sick leave
◆ Use object pronouns

Why do sick people need to stay home?

leave
terrible

◆ **Reading Tip** Look at the title before you read. What does the title tell you about Jim?

Sick at Work

Today is Monday. Jim's sick.

He's at work. He feels terrible.

He coughs and sneezes. He asks Mary for aspirin.

The other people at work don't want to get sick.

They want him to go home.

He wants to stay. He has a big meeting at 2:00.

Speak or Circle

1. Is Jim OK?   Yes   No

2. Is he at home?   Yes   No

3. Are the other people unhappy?   Yes   No

4. Is Mary at work?   Yes   No

5. Does Jim want to go home?   Yes   No

Class Chat Walk around. Ask questions. Write answers in your chart.

When you have a cold, what are your symptoms?

I sneeze. I have a headache.

Name	When you have a _cold_, what are your symptoms?	What do you take for it?
Maria	sneeze, a headache	aspirin

Vocabulary

Listen. Repeat. Circle and write new words.

cough

sneeze

tissue

give

aspirin

cough drops

cough syrup

_____
your word

Grammar Talk: Object Pronouns

Aspirin helps **me** feel better.

The doctor can see **you** tomorrow.

Can you take **him** home?

Call **her** at work.

Buy **it** at the drugstore.

Can you see **us** today?

Can you take **them**?

Tanya gives **a cough drop** to **Jim**. She gives **it** to **him**.

Where do object pronouns go in a sentence? Talk to your teacher about this question.

Activity A **Class Chat Follow-Up** Look at your Class Chat chart. Write sentences in your notebook.

<u>When Maria has a cold, she sneezes and has a headache.</u>
<u>She takes aspirin.</u>

Activity B   Change the **word** to an object pronoun.
Read the sentence to your partner.

1. Maria takes **aspirin** for a headache.

<u>Maria takes it for a headache.</u>

2. Michael asks **Susan** for a tissue.

_____

3. John has **tissues** on his desk.

_____

4. Please give **John** some cough drops.

_____

Remember?

Subject	Object
I ⟶	me
you ⟶	you
he ⟶	him
she ⟶	her
it ⟶	it
they ⟶	them

Activity C   One partner reads the sentence. The other partner
reads the sentence with subject and object pronouns. Both partners
write the new sentence with pronouns.

1. **Jim** talks to **Mary**.   <u>He talks to her.</u>

2. **Mary** tells **Jim** to go home. _____

3. **Jim** has a meeting with **Mr. and Mrs. Mankin.** _____

4. **The meeting** is very important to **Jim.** _____

5. **Jim** writes a note to **Mrs. Ramirez.** _____

TASK 1 Ask to Leave Early

With a partner, role-play a conversation with your boss or teacher.
Tell why you are leaving work or school.

Writing Extension   Write a note. Your note tells why you need to leave work or
school. Read your note to your partner.

Making a Doctor's Appointment

- ◆ Fill out a medical form
- ◆ Use *be* in *Wh-* questions

receptionist

Why do you call the doctor?

◆ **Listening Tip** 🎧 Listen to your teacher or the audio. Take notes when you listen. Write important information. You can read the words on page 118.

Jim calls the doctor.

Speak or Circle

1. Jim calls
    a. an appointment.
    b. the doctor.
    c. sick.
    d. tomorrow.

2. Jim feels
    a. fever.
    b. sick.
    c. headache.
    d. throat.

3. Jim has
    a. a note.
    b. a stomachache.
    c. a sore throat.
    d. an aspirin.

4. Jim's appointment is
    a. tomorrow at noon.
    b. Sunday at 3:00.
    c. tomorrow at 3:00.
    d. today at 4:00.

Class Chat
Walk around. Ask questions. Write answers in your chart. Talk about your doctor.

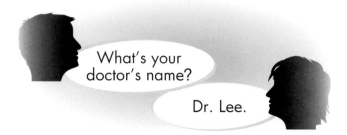

Name	What's your doctor's name?	Where's your doctor's office?
Niki	Dr. Lee	On Park Road.

Activity A
Class Chat Follow-Up Look at your Class Chat chart. Write sentences in your notebook.

Niki's doctor is Dr. Lee. His office is on Park Road.

Vocabulary
Listen. Repeat. Circle and write new words.

how

what

when

where

who

why

appointment

doctor

office

temperature

hurt

_____
your word

Grammar Talk: Present-Tense *Wh-* Questions with *Be*

		(Contraction)		
Why	**am**		I hot?	You have a fever.
How	**are**		your children?	They're sick.
Where	**is**	(Where's)	the aspirin?	It's in the cabinet.
Who	**is**	(Who's)	your doctor?	He's Dr. Ramos.
When	**is**	(When's)	your appointment?	It's tomorrow.
What	**is**	(What's)	your temperature?	It's 101°.

Where is the question word? What form of be *is in contractions? What letter is missing in the contraction?*

98.6° = normal temperature

Activity B Jim is at the doctor's office. He needs to fill out a medical information form. Write the questions.

	Please Print
1. Last Name **Martin**	First Name **James**
2. Address **1650 Teal Avenue, San Francisco, CA 94119**	3. Date of birth **3-12-75**
4. Phone Number: Day **(415) 555-8437** Evening **(415) 555-2334**	
5. Employer: **Pacific Bank**	6. Address: **349 Gray Street, San Francisco, CA 94112**
7. Allergies? Medicine: **penicillin** Other: **cats**	8. Reason for this visit? **sore throat, fever**

1. Why/Jim/doctor's office/today? <u>Why is Jim at the doctor's office today?</u>

2. Where/Jim's office? _____

3. When/Jim's birthday? _____

4. What/his allergies? _____

5. What/his/phone numbers? _____

6. What/Jim's/last name? _____

Exchange papers with your partner. Check your partner's work.
One partner asks a question. One answers. Write the answers.
Check your answers with your partner.

TASK 2 Give Medical Information

Use the form above. Talk to your partner. Give information about you for questions 1 to 4 on the form. Ask your partner questions 1 to 4. Tell the class about your partner.

Take Your Medicine!

◆ Read medicine labels
◆ Use *Wh-* questions with other verbs

What medicines are in your medicine cabinet?

exceed
Exp. = expires
minor
relieve

◆ **Reading Tip** When you read labels, look for important words in **bold print** or color. Read the medicine labels.

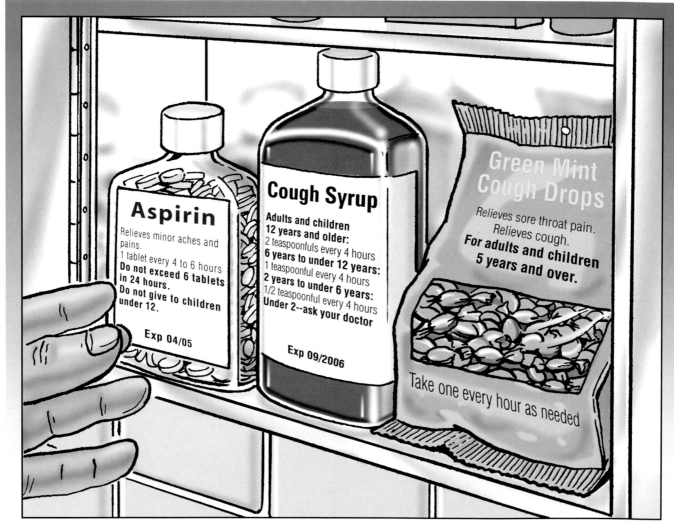

Aspirin
Relieves minor aches and pains.
1 tablet every 4 to 6 hours
Do not exceed 6 tablets in 24 hours.
Do not give to children under 12.

Exp 04/05

Cough Syrup
Adults and children
12 years and older:
2 teaspoonfuls every 4 hours
6 years to under 12 years:
1 teaspoonful every 4 hours
2 years to under 6 years:
1/2 teaspoonful every 4 hours
Under 2--ask your doctor

Exp 09/2006

Green Mint Cough Drops
Relieves sore throat pain.
Relieves cough.
For adults and children 5 years and over.

Take one every hour as needed

Jim looks in his medicine cabinet. "What's good for a cough?"

Talk or Write

1. How much cough syrup can Jim take?
2. How many aspirin can Jim take in 24 hours?

Class Chat
Walk around. Ask questions. Write answers in your chart.

Where do you buy medicine?

In a drugstore.

Name	What medicine do you take for a cold?	Where do you buy medicine?
Inez	aspirin	at Good Foods Supermarket

Activity A
Class Chat Follow-Up Look at your Class Chat chart. Write sentences in your notebook.

<u>Inez takes aspirin for a cold. She buys it at Good Foods Supermarket.</u>

Vocabulary

Listen. Repeat. Circle and write new words.

directions

expiration

label

warning

dose

maximum

tablet

teaspoonful (tsp.)

pain

drugstore

remedy

Grammar Talk:
Present-Tense *Wh*- Questions with Other Verbs

How	do	I take this medicine?	Read the directions.
When	do	you see the doctor?	I see him tomorrow.
What	do	we need at the store?	You need cough syrup.
Why	do	they need aspirin?	They have headaches.
Where	does	Dr. Lee work?	He works at the clinic.
Who	does	Jim call?	He calls his boss.

Where is the question word? What word comes after the question word? Talk to your teacher about these questions.

Pronunciation Target • Intonation with *Be* and *Wh*- Questions
🎧 *Listen to your teacher or the audio.*

Is your appointment at 3:00 P.M.?↑   When is your appointment?↓

Activity B Look at the medicine label. Write information in the chart. Use this label and the labels on page 54.

TUMMY EASE

For a Stomachache

Dose: Take 2 to 4 tablets as needed.

Daily Maximum: 16 tablets

Warning: Do not use maximum dose for more than 2 weeks.

Exp. Date Nov/2008

Medicine	Tummy Ease	Aspirin	Cough Syrup	Cough Drops
Dose	2-4 tablets			
How Often	as needed			
Daily Maximum	16			
Warning	no more than 2 weeks			
Expiration	Nov/2008			

Talk with a partner. Do all medicine labels have the same information? What is different?

daily

How often?

different

same

In the US   Home Remedies

Not everybody needs a doctor when they are sick.
Some people use home remedies.
They drink hot tea for a sore throat.
They eat chicken soup for a cold or the flu.

☛ Compare Cultures

What home remedies do you use in your home country? Talk.

What do you do for a cold?

I make chicken soup.

soup

tea

TASK 3 Talk About Medicines

What are three medicines in your home? Make a chart like the one in Activity B. Talk to your group about your chart.

Family Medical Information Form

Do these things to complete the Family Medical Information Form.

Get Ready

Do these things:

- Get your medical information and your family's medical information.
- Make a list of the addresses where you and your family are during the day.
- Make a list of the phone numbers.

Do the Work

Use the Family Medical Information Forms from your teacher:

- Complete one form for you.
- Complete forms for people in your family.

Present Your Project

- Make copies of your forms. Keep the forms at home. Give a copy to each family member. Give a copy to your neighbor.
- Practice the phone conversations with a partner.

Date:	For the <blank line> Family		
Address:			
Cross Streets:			
Phone Number:			
Insurance Company:			
Policy Number:			

Important Family Information: *Make a copy for each family member.*

Family Member:			
Birthdate:			
	(Month)	(Day)	(Year)
School/Work Address:			
School/Work Phone No:			
Medical Problems:			

neighbor

When you call a doctor: "Hello. This is _____. I need to make an appointment. I have a _____."

When you call your children's school: "Hello. This is _____. My son/daughter, _____, is sick today."

When you call work: "Hello. This is _____. I'm sick today."

✏️💻 Technology Extra

Call and leave a message for the teacher. Say you are sick today.

I Need a Budget!

Making a Budget

Home
1

Work/School
2

Community
3

◆ **Vocabulary** Money problems • Job skills
  • Shopping for clothes

◆ **Language** Present continuous statements and questions
  • *Like, like to, need, need to, want, want to* • *This, that, these, those*

◆ **Pronunciation** Long and short e sounds

◆ **Culture** Customer service

borrow

insurance

utilities

MY BUDGET- APRIL 2004	
SALARY	$ 1300
TIPS	$ 100
TOTAL INCOME	$1400
EXPENSES	
Rent	$ 550
Gas for car	$ 100
Utilities	$ 75
Phone	$ 130
Car Insurance	$ 45
Food	$ 160
Credit card	$ 50
For Mother	$ 150
TOTAL EXPENSES	$ 1260
$$ REMAINING	$ 140

When do you pay your bills?

Ramon is from Mexico. He lives in Michigan now. He works hard. But he doesn't have much money.

Think and Talk

1. What do you see?
2. What's the problem?
3. What do you do when you need money?

What's Your Opinion? Is it OK to ask friends or family for money?

❏ Always   ❏ Sometimes   ❏ Never

Picture Dictionary   Listen. Repeat. Circle new words. Write the words.

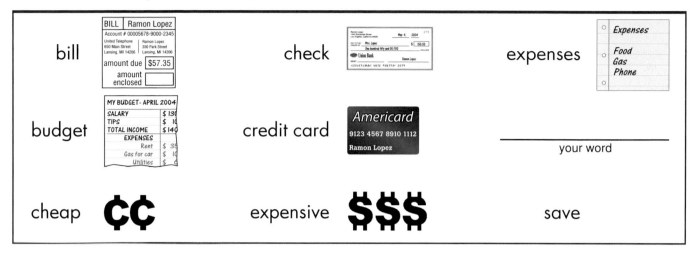

bill

check

expenses

budget

credit card

_____
your word

cheap ¢¢

expensive $$$

save

Gather Your Thoughts   How do you save money? Make an idea map. Here's an example.

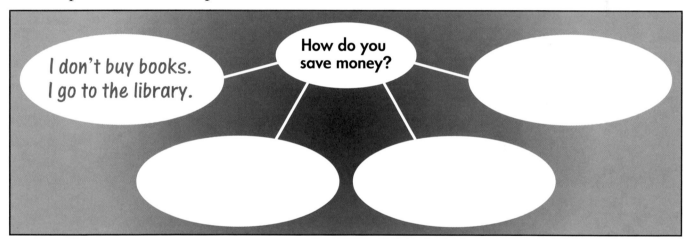

I don't buy books. I go to the library.

How do you save money?

What's the Problem?   Look at the words in the Picture Dictionary. What do you think? Is it easy or difficult to save money in the US? Think or talk with a partner.

Setting Goals   Check ✔ your budgeting goals.

❏ **1.** Learn ways to save money.
❏ **2.** Make a budget.
❏ **3.** Talk about things you want, need, and like.
❏ **4.** Return something you buy.
❏ **5.** Another goal: _____

Thinking about Saving Money

◆ Learn ways to save money
◆ Use present-continuous tense

What bills do you pay?

◆ **Reading Tip** Try to guess the meaning of new words. What do you think Ramon is writing about?

easy
journal
might
more
quit
rent
study

April 21
I work in a restaurant now.
I'm taking an English class at an adult school in the mornings.
The students in my class are from many countries.
We are studying about jobs in the US now.
I might quit school. I need more work.
I need to send more money to my mother.
I have a lot of bills.
I pay a lot of money for rent and other things.
I'm trying to save money, but it's not easy.

Ramon is writing in his journal.

Talk or Write

1. Where does Ramon work?
2. Why does Ramon think he might quit school?
3. Why does he need more work?
4. What does he pay money for?
5. What is Ramon trying to do?

Class Chat Walk around. Ask questions. Write answers in the idea map from your teacher. How are you saving money in your community, at work, and at home?

How are you saving money at work?

I make lunch to take to work.

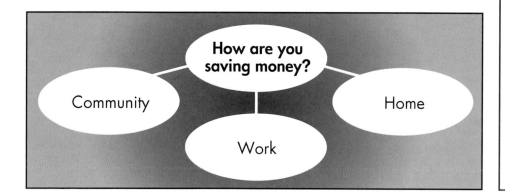

How are you saving money?

Community

Work

Home

Vocabulary

Listen. Repeat. Circle and write new words.

e-mail

phone

rent

restaurant

utilities

pay

spend

try

a lot of = many

Grammar Talk: Present-Continuous Statements and Questions

Subject	*Be*	(Contraction)	
I	am	(I'm)	buy**ing** clothes for work.
You	are	(You're)	tak**ing** an English class.
He	is	(He's)	liv**ing** with two friends.
She	is	(She's)	study**ing** English.
We	are	(We're)	try**ing** to save money.
You	are	(You're)	work**ing** a lot of hours.
They	are	(They're)	plann**ing** to register for class.

Questions

	He	is	work**ing**.	
Is	he		work**ing**	at the store now? Yes, he **is**.
Where	is	he	work**ing**?	at the store

What ending do you add to the main verb to make the present continuous? Talk about the answer to this question with your teacher.

Activity A Choose one word from each column. Write sentences about the pictures in your notebook.

She	am	renting	her mother.
He	is	e-mailing	the bill.
They	are	saving	five dollars.
I		paying	a video.

1.
2.
3.
4.

Read the sentences to your partner. Exchange papers with your partner. Check your partner's work.

Activity B Who is saving money today? Look at the pictures of Hector and his friend, Ken. Write sentences in your notebook. What are Hector and Ken doing?

1. Ken
2. Hector
3. Ken
4. Hector

How can Ken save money? Talk with the students in your class.

TASK 1 I'm Spending a Lot of Money

Work with a partner. Share information. What are you spending a lot of money on? Tell your partner how you can save money. Make a list.

I'm calling Russia a lot. To save money, I can use e-mail.

Make a poster of how to save money. Put it on the wall in your classroom.

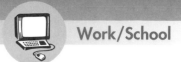
Improving Your Job Skills

- ◆ Talk and write about needs and wants
- ◆ Use *need, want,* and *like*
- ◆ Use *need to, want to,* and *like to*

| customers |
| first |
| improve |
| service |
| tip |

What kind of service do you want at a restaurant?

◆ **Listening Tip** 🎧 Listen for details. What is Mr. Martin telling Ramon? You can read the words on page 119.

Talk or Write

1. What does Ramon want?
2. What does he need to improve?
3. What do happy customers give?
4. What does Ramon thank Mr. Martin for?

What's Your Opinion? Is it OK to speak English at home or with your friends?

❑ Always   ❑ Sometimes   ❑ Never

Class Chat Walk around. Ask questions. Write answers in your chart.

Name	Where do you need to speak English?	Where do you like to speak your native language?
Jenny	at work	at home

Activity A **Class Chat Follow-Up** Look at your class chat chart. Write sentences in your notebook.

<u>Jenny needs to speak English at work.</u>

Vocabulary

Listen. Repeat. Circle and write new words.

improve

wear

practice

service

speak

better

too much

Grammar Talk:
Like and *Like To, Need* and *Need To, Want* and *Want To*

Ramon **likes his job.**	He **likes to work** at the restaurant.
Ramon **needs more hours** at work.	He **needs to ask** his boss.
The customers **want good service.**	They **want to talk** to their waiter now.

What follows want, need, *and* like? *What verb form follows* want to, need to, *and* like to? *Talk about the answers to these questions with your teacher.*

Pronunciation Target • Long and Short *e* Sounds

🎧 *Listen to your teacher or the audio.*

cheap   e-mail   need   rent   spend   expensive

Activity B What do you want at school or work? What do you want to do? Write two answers for *want* and two answers for *want to* in your notebook.

Want	**Want to**
1. I want better tips.	I want to use the computer.

Read your sentences to your partner. Listen to your partner's sentences. Tell another person in your group about your partner.

He wants better tips.

Activity C What do you like at school or work? What do you like to do? Write two answers for *like* and two answers for *like to* in your notebook.

Like	**Like to**
1. I like the people.	I like to talk to the customers.

Read your sentences to your partner. Listen to your partner's sentences. Tell another person in your group about your partner.

Ken likes to talk to the customers.

TASK 2 Make a Change

What do you want to change? With a partner, ask and answer questions about things that you want to change. Write your partner's answers in the chart. Then tell your partner what to do. Write your advice.

What do you want to change?

I want to get a better job.

You need to improve your English.

Name	What do you want to change?	You need to _____.
Sonali	job	improve your English

Shopping for Clothes

◆ Read shopping ads
◆ Use *this, that, these, those*

Where do you shop for clothes?

◆ **Reading Tip**   Read the Talk or Write questions. Then read the ads for answers.

size:
small
medium
large
price
clothing

Men's Clothing

Sweaters
$25.99
S-XL green,
blue

T-Shirts
$12.99
black,
white, red
Sizes S, M, L

Shoes
*Buy one pair and
get one pair free!*

Kid's athletic
shoes
$39.99

Men's
athletic shoes
$49.99

Sale August 4-14

Men's Shirts

Men's long-sleeved shirts
blue/red/
green
M, L
$25.00
Now
$12.50

Prices good Sunday,
8/8 to Saturday, 8/14.

Talk or Write

1. What's on sale?
2. When are the men's shoes on sale?
3. How much do you save on men's shirts?
4. What's the price of the T-shirts?

Class Chat
Walk around. Talk to the students in your class. Ask questions. Write answers in your chart.

What color is that shirt?

This shirt is red.

What color are those shoes?

These shoes are black.

Name	What color...?
Lisa	This shirt is red. These shoes are black.

Remember?

white	red	orange	yellow	green	blue	black

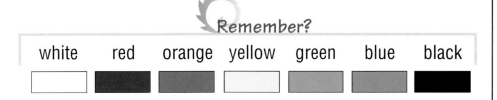

Grammar Talk: *This, That, These, Those*

I need to	return	**this**	blue shirt.
I need to	see	**that**	coat.
I want to	try on	**these**	sweaters.
I want to	buy	**those**	black shoes.

What words do you use for things near you? What words do you use for things not near you? Talk to your teacher about these questions.

Vocabulary

Listen. Repeat. Circle and write new words.

clothes

dress

pants

shirt

shoes

sweater

T-shirt

fit

return

try on

long

loose

short

tight

on sale

sale

_____

your word

Activity A 🎧 Listen to your teacher or the audio. Use the words in the box to complete the conversation.

black	✔ need to	shirt	these	this

Ramon: I _____need to_____ return _____ shirts.
  ₁ ₂

Salesperson: What's the problem?

Ramon: They don't fit well. Is that _____ on sale?
  ₃

Salesperson: No, it isn't. _____ shirt is on sale.
  ₄

Ramon: Good! I need a medium in _____.
  ₅

Salesperson: OK. Anything else?

Ramon: No, thanks. That's it for today.

> **Idiom Watch!**
> *That's it. =*
> *That's all I*
> *need.*

Activity B   Role-play with your partner. One is a salesperson. One is a customer. The customer is returning clothes to the store. Use vocabulary words.

> customer

Can I help you?   Yes. I'm returning these shoes. They're too tight.

In the US   Customer Service

The customer is always right!
In the US, stores want to sell things.
They want customers to be happy.

☛ Compare Cultures

Is good service important in your country?

❑ Yes

❑ Sometimes

❑ No

TASK 3   It Doesn't Fit!

Look at Activity A. Think of something you need to return.
Make a conversation with your partner. Write the conversation.
Role-play the conversation.

Make a Budget

Do these things to plan, make, and present a budget.

Get Ready

With your partner, do these things:
- Look at Ramon's old budget on page 58. Look at Ramon's new budget.
- Ken is living with Ramon now. They are sharing expenses.
- How is Ramon saving money now?
- How can he save more money?

Do the Work

Think about your budget.
Use the budget form from your teacher.
- Complete the budget form for you.
- How are you saving money now?
- How can you save more money?

Present Your Project

With your group, talk about your budget.
- Ask your group, "How can I save more money?"
- Write on the board one way your group says you can save money.

June 2004		How Ramon is saving money	How Ramon is making more money	How can Ramon save more money?
Salary	$1500			
Tips	$300		better service	
Total Income	$1800			
Expenses				
Rent	$275	getting a roommate		
Gas for car	$100			
Utilities	$37.50	getting a roommate		
Phone	$130			
Car Insurance	$45			
Food	$160			
Credit card	$50			
For Mother	$150			
Total Expenses	$947.50			
$$ Remaining	$852.50			

✂🖥 Technology Extra
Do you need to buy something? Ask your teacher for a web site. Find the price.
Talk with your partner.

What's for Dinner?

Choosing Good Food

Community 1

Home 2

Work/School 3

◆ **Vocabulary** Foods • Coupons

◆ **Language** Count and noncount nouns • *There is* and *there are* • Questions and answers with *or*

◆ **Pronunciation** Intonation with words in a list

◆ **Culture** Fast food

Do all the people in your family like the same food?

Miyako and her family are hungry.
They want different things to eat.

Think and Talk

1. What do you see?
2. What's the problem?
3. What do you like to eat for dinner?

Picture Dictionary Listen. Repeat. Circle new words. Write the words.

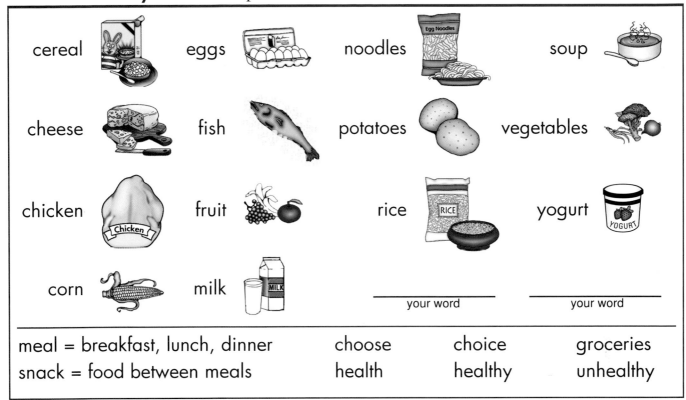

cereal	eggs	noodles	soup
cheese	fish	potatoes	vegetables
chicken	fruit	rice	yogurt
corn	milk	your word	your word

meal = breakfast, lunch, dinner   choose   choice   groceries
snack = food between meals   health   healthy   unhealthy

Gather Your Thoughts When do you eat the foods in the pictures?

Make an idea map. Write the foods you eat. Here is an example.

Foods I Eat — Breakfast — Lunch — Snack — Dinner

What's the Problem? Is it easy to get healthy food in the US?

Are your meals healthy? Think or talk with a partner.

Setting Goals Check ✔ your food goals.

❏ **1.** Plan meals.
❏ **2.** Eat healthy food.
❏ **3.** Save money on food.
❏ **4.** Make healthy meals my family likes.
❏ **5.** Ask for foods at restaurants or stores.
❏ **6.** Another goal: _____

At the Supermarket

- Ask for help
- Use count and noncount nouns

aisle
each
flyer
section
specials

How do you find food in a supermarket?

◆ **Reading Tip** Always read the title of the flyer first.

Today's Specials

PRODUCE Aisle 11	DAIRY Aisle 7	BAKERY Aisle 6	MEAT Aisle 3
Fresh Corn 3 for $1	Butter 3 lbs. for $6	French Bread 1 loaf for $1.49	Whole Chicken $3.99 each
Red Apples 3 lbs. for $3	Yogurt 5 cups for $3	Cookies 10-oz. bag for $2.99	Steak 1 lb. for $3.49
	Swiss Cheese 1 lb. for $2.89		
	Onion Dip 1 pint for $2		
	Non-fat Milk 1 gal. for $2.29		

I need to find these five things.

Talk or Write

1. Where is Miyako?
2. What does she want to buy?
3. Where are the apples?
4. Where is the bread?

Picture Dictionary Listen. Repeat. Circle new words. Write the words.

apples   bread   cookies   steak

bananas   butter   lettuce   tomatoes

bakery   dairy   meat   produce

Partner Chat Look at "Today's Specials" on page 72. With your partner, ask and answer questions. Write answers in your chart.

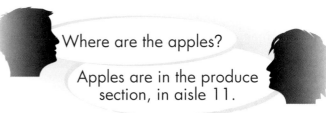

Where are the apples?

Apples are in the produce section, in aisle 11.

Food	Section	Aisle
Apples	Produce	11

Grammar Talk: Count and Noncount Nouns

Count Nouns	Noncount Nouns
Apples are in the produce section.	**Chicken is** in the meat section.
Cookies are not in the produce section.	**Corn is** not in the meat section.
Tomatoes are on sale.	**Milk is** in aisle 7.

Count nouns *name things you can count, like apples.* Noncount nouns *name things you cannot count, like chicken. What verb is used with* apples? *With* chicken?

Pronunciation Target • Intonation with Words in a List

🎧 *Listen to your teacher or the audio.*

The store has <u>apples,</u>↑ <u>eggs,</u>↑ <u>bananas,</u>↑ and <u>corn</u>↓ on sale.

Activity A Read the sign. Talk with a partner.

How much are the carrots?

They are $1.59 a bag.

How much is the lettuce?

It's $1.00.

THIS WEEK ONLY

Carrots	$1.59 a bag	Mushrooms	$2.99 a basket
Lettuce	$1.00 a head	Strawberries	$1.99 a basket
Potatoes	$2.00 a bag	Bananas	$2.49 a bunch

a dozen = 12
a bag
a basket
a bunch
a head
grocery
mushroom
strawberry

Activity B Look at "Today's Specials" on page 72. Complete the sentences.

1. **Miyako:** Excuse me, where _____ the apples?

2. **Clerk:** They are in aisle 11, in the _____ section.

3. **Miyako:** Thank you. And where _____ the bread?

4. **Clerk:** It's in aisle 6, in the _____ section.

5. **Miyako:** Thank you. _____ corn on sale?

6. **Clerk:** Yes, it is on _____ this weekend only.

Read the sentences to your partner. Listen to your partner.

TASK 1 Write a Grocery List

Produce	Meat	Bakery	Dairy	Other
			Milk	

What foods do you buy at the store? Write the names of the foods. Then tell a partner. Your partner writes the words in the chart. Help your partner spell the words.

One Step Up
Ask a clerk for help.
Use your chart.
Student A: Excuse me. Where can I find *milk*?
Student B: In the *dairy* section.
Student A: Thank you.

 Home

Saving Money on Food

◆ Read coupons
◆ Use *there is* and *there are*

chips
hungry
soda
visit
worried
television

How can you eat healthy food and save money?

◆ **Reading Tip** Read the title. Read the Talk or Write questions. Then read the story.

Miyako's Children

Miyako has two children. The children are always hungry after school.

Their friends often visit. They watch television and do homework.

There are bags of chips and cookies on the floor. There are soda cans on the table.

The snacks are not healthy. They are expensive. Miyako is worried.

Talk or Write

1. What are the children eating?
2. Why are they eating?
3. Why is Miyako worried?

Class Chat

Class Chat How do you save money on groceries? Ask and answer. Complete the chart. Then write sentences in your notebook.

What's your name?	How do you save money on food?
Miyako	I use coupons.

Miyako saves money. She uses coupons.

How do you save money on food?

I use coupons.

Vocabulary

Listen. Repeat. Circle and write new words.

coupon

savings

magazine

newspaper

worried

hungry

Grammar Talk: *There Is* and *There Are*

There is a special today.	
Is there a special today?	<u>Yes</u>, **there is.**
There is a food coupon in the magazine.	
Is there a food coupon in your apartment?	<u>No</u>, **there isn't.**
There are food coupons in magazines in the US.	
Are there food coupons in magazines in your country?	<u>Yes</u>, **there are.**
There are food coupons in the newspaper.	
Are there food coupons in the phone book?	<u>No</u>, **there aren't.**

Use there is *with singular nouns. Use* there are *with plural nouns.*

Activity A

Activity A Miyako sees her friend, John, leaving the supermarket. Put the conversation in order. Number 1 to 5.

> **One Step Up**
> Read the conversation with a partner.

_____ **John:** You can buy six ears of corn for a dollar.

_____ **Miyako:** I'm fine, thanks. Is there anything on sale today?

_____ **John:** Yes, there are great savings with these coupons.

_____ **Miyako:** Is there fresh corn on sale?

__1__ **John:** Hi, Miyako. How are you today?

Activity B Read the coupons. Answer the questions.

MANUFACTURER'S COUPON
EXPIRES 5-19-05

SAVE 25¢
When you buy any 32-oz. Yogurt

YOGURT

MANUFACTURER'S COUPON   EXPIRES 3-31-05

SAVE $1.00 on any 5
Tomatoes 14.5 oz. or larger
Limit one coupon per purchase.

Tomatoes

expires = cannot be used after this date
expiration date = date when coupon expires
limit = no more than

1. Is there a limit on the tomato coupon? __Yes, there is._____

2. Is there an expiration date on the yogurt coupon? _____

3. Are there expiration dates on the two coupons? _____

Read the questions and answers with a partner.

TASK 2 Look for Specials and Coupons

Work in your group.

What foods do you need in your homes?

Make a list for your group.

Find specials or coupons for the foods.

Tell about the specials and coupons.

This coupon has an expiration date.

There is a special on eggs this week.

It's Lunch Time!

◆ Order food in fast-food restaurants

◆ Use *or* in questions and answers

Where do you eat lunch?

cafeteria
burgers = hamburgers
fries = french fries

◆ **Listening Tip** 🎧 When you listen, look first. Think about what's happening. Look at the photo. Think. What's happening with Miyako and her friends at school? Listen to your teacher or the audio. You can read the words on page 119.

Miyako and her friends make lunch choices.

Talk or Write

1. Where is Miyako?
2. Where are her friends going?

What's Your Opinion? Should Miyako go with her friends?

❑ Yes   ❑ Maybe   ❑ No

Class Chat   Walk around. Ask a question about food. Use *or* and the food words on pages 71 and 73. Write answers in the chart. Then write sentences in your notebook.

What do you eat for lunch?

I eat noodles or potatoes.

What's your name?	What do you eat for lunch?
Blanca	noodles or potatoes

<u>Blanca eats noodles or potatoes for lunch.</u>

Grammar Talk: Questions and Answers with *Or*

Do you eat lunch at home **or** at work?
I eat lunch at work.

Where do you buy your food?
I buy it at Happy Mart **or** at Smart Shop.

Use or *to talk about choices.*

⭐ **In the US**   Busy People, Fast Food

People in the US are very busy. They often don't have time to buy or cook food. At school or at work they are far from home. Fast food is popular.

☞ **Compare Cultures**

What do busy people eat in your home country?
Is fast food popular? Talk to people in your group.

Vocabulary

Listen. Repeat. Circle and write new words.

fast food

popular

cook

deliver

eat out

for here

to go

french fries (fries)

hamburgers (burgers)

salad

_____
your word

busy
far
popular

Activity A 🎧 Listen to your teacher or the audio. Read.

buy	choices	cook	Fast food	health	healthy

People in the US are very busy. They often don't have time to

_____ or _____ food. At school or at work they are
1   2

far from home. _____ is popular. But there are problems with fast
3

food. It often has a lot of fat, salt, or sugar. Too much fat, salt, and sugar are bad

for people's _____ . Some fast-food restaurants are changing. Now
4

they have salads or other _____ foods. Small changes in food
5

_____ can make big health differences.
5

Listen again. Choose words from the box. Complete the sentences.

Activity B 🎧 Listen to your teacher or the audio. Read the sentences. Circle *True* or *False*.

1. Maria is at the Hamburger Hut.   True   False
2. She orders three meals.   True   False
3. Maria wants a soda.   True   False
4. She wants to eat lunch at the restaurant.   True   False
5. Her meal is $4.45.   True   False

TASK 3   Find Fast-Food Restaurants

Talk in your group. Are there fast-food restaurants in your
neighborhoods? Make a chart.

One Step Up
Write phone numbers in your chart. Check ✔ the restaurants that deliver food.

Fast-Food Restaurant	Kind of Food	Expensive?	Healthy?
Burger House	hamburger	no	sometimes

Planning a Meal

Do these things to plan, prepare, and present a meal.

Get Ready

Do these things:
- Find a recipe. Write it on the form from your teacher.
- What do you need to buy? Make a list of foods.
- Check the newspaper for food ads and coupons.

If you don't have time or can't cook, make choices:
- Can you order this food in a restaurant?
- Is it expensive in a restaurant?

Do the Work

If you have time and can cook:
- Buy the foods for the recipe.
- Make the food.
- Eat the food. Share it with family or friends.

If you don't have time or can't cook:
- Order restaurant food to go or to eat in the restaurant.
- What's in the food? Make a list.
- Write how much the food costs.
- Eat the food. Share it with family or friends.

Remember?

cheap ¢ ¢

expensive $ $ $

share

Present Your Project

Talk or write about your food:
- Is it from a recipe or a restaurant?
- Read your food shopping list.
- Is the food healthy? Tell why or why not.
- Is the food cheap or expensive? Tell why or why not.
- Tell why you and your family like the food.

One Step Up

Have a class party. Bring your food. Eat new foods. Talk about the foods. Talk about food in the US and other places. Have fun.

Technology Extra

Write your recipe on the computer. Make copies for the class.

Call the Police!

Reporting a Crime

Home
1

Community
2

Work/School
3

◆ **Vocabulary** Home inventory words • Police report words • Describing people

◆ **Language** Past-tense statements with *be* • Past-tense statements with regular and irregular verbs • Past-tense questions with *be* and other verbs

◆ **Pronunciation** Long and short *i* sounds • Past-tense ending sounds

◆ **Culture** Neighborhood Watch programs in the US

important

Are your things safe?

Sara's a nurse at a hospital. She's going home. What is happening at her home?

Think and Talk

1. What's the problem?
2. Is your neighborhood safe?

What's Your Opinion? Is it important to buy insurance for your things?

❏ Always ❏ Sometimes ❏ Never

Picture Dictionary   Listen. Repeat. Circle new words. Write the words.

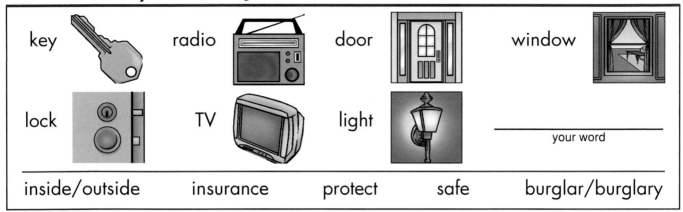

key   radio   door   window

lock   TV   light   _____
                                          your word

inside/outside   insurance   protect   safe   burglar/burglary

Gather Your Thoughts   How do you protect your things?

Make an idea map. Here's an example.

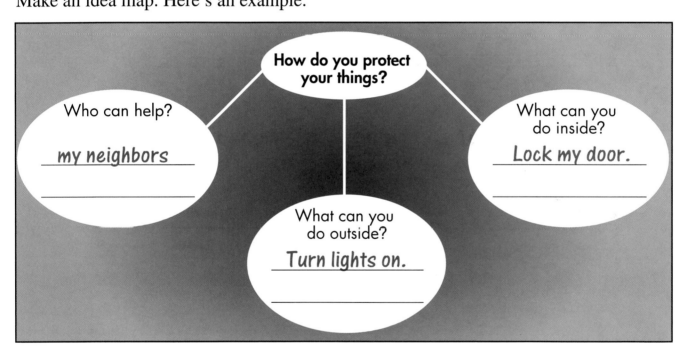

How do you protect
your things?

Who can help?

my neighbors
_____

What can you
do inside?

Lock my door.
_____

What can you
do outside?

Turn lights on.
_____

What's the Problem?   Is it easy to protect your things? Look

at the words in the Picture Dictionary. Think or talk to a partner.

Setting Goals   Check ✔ your safety goals.

❑ **1.** Talk to the police.

❑ **2.** Report what happened.

❑ **3.** Fill out a form.

❑ **4.** Talk about protecting your things.

❑ **5.** Describe someone.

❑ **6.** Another goal: _____

What a Mess!

◆ Take a home inventory
◆ Use the past tense with *be*

Is your home safe?

missing
shocked

◆ **Reading Tip** Look at the end marks, like ., !, ?. What do they tell you about the story?

Sara's Apartment

It was Wednesday night.

It was very late.
Sara was shocked when she got home.

Her apartment was dark. The light was not on.

Her apartment door was open!

Where was the computer?

Where were the TV and VCR? They were missing!

Books, photos, and papers were on the floor.

It was a burglary!

Talk or Write
1. Why was Sara shocked?
2. What was missing?
3. What was on the floor?

Now	Before
is	was
are	were

Class Chat
Walk around. Ask questions. Write answers in your chart.

> What things in your home are important to you?

> My family dishes.

Name	What things in your home are important to you?	What things were important to you in your home country?
Sofia	My family dishes.	My books and photos.

Activity A
Class Chat Follow-Up Look at your chart. Write sentences in your notebook.

Sofia's family dishes are important to her. Her books and photos were important in her home country.

Vocabulary
Listen. Repeat. Circle and write new words.

- important
- replace
- photo album
- computer
- VCR
- dark
- light
- locked
- quiet
- mess

Grammar Talk: Past-Tense Statements with *Be*

Subject	Verb		Subject	Verb + *not*	(Contraction)	
I	was	at school.	I	was not	(wasn't)	at work.
He/She	was	at work.	He/She	was not	(wasn't)	at school.
It	was	rainy.	It	was not	(wasn't)	sunny.
You	were	at home.	You	were not	(weren't)	at the store.
We	were	in New York.	We	were not	(weren't)	in Reno.
The dishes	were	expensive.	They	were not	(weren't)	cheap.

What word makes the verb negative? What letter is missing in the contraction? Talk to your teacher about these questions.

Pronunciation Target • Long and Short *i* Sounds
🎧 *Listen to your teacher or the audio.*

quiet   night   crime   window   missing   important

Activity B   With a partner, change the verb to past tense.

1. Sara is at work.   <u>Sara was at work.</u>

2. It is Wednesday night.   _____

3. It is a burglary.   _____

4. Where are her TV and VCR?   _____

Activity C   How do you protect your home? Check the boxes.

1. ❏ doors locked   ❏ doors open
2. ❏ light on   ❏ light off
3. ❏ one lock   ❏ two locks
4. ❏ key inside   ❏ key outside
5. ❏ window open   ❏ window closed
6. ❏ radio on   ❏ radio off

Activity D   Work with a partner. Use the words in the box
to complete the story.

burglary	computer	✔ family	important	replace

Sara has photos of her family in a book. She has a lot of _____<u>family</u>_____
                                                                    1
photos. Sara has other things in the book too. There are

letters from family and friends. But the photo album is a mess.

Sara also lost her computer in the _____. A _____ is
                                            2   3
expensive. But Sara can _____ the computer. The photo album is
                                  4
not expensive. But it is _____ to her.
                                5

TASK 1   Take a Home Inventory

Make a list of things in your home. What things were expensive?
What things are important to you? Why? Can you replace these things?

Talking to the Police

◆ Report a crime
◆ Use past-tense verbs

ever
van

Did you ever need to talk to the police?

◆ **Listening Tip** 🎧 Listen to your teacher or the audio. You can read the words on page 119. Listen for the words that tell time or sequence: *first* and *then*.

Sara talks to the police.

Talk or Write

1. What happened at 9:50?
2. When did Sara come home?
3. What was missing?
4. Who saw the burglar?

What's Your Opinion? Do you help your neighbors protect their things?

❏ Always   ❏ Sometimes   ❏ Never

Idiom Watch!
fill out =
complete the
information

Class Chat Walk around. Ask questions. Write answers in your chart.

What did the burglars take?

They took my bike.

Name	Were you or was someone you know ever robbed?	What did the burglars take?
Jose	Yes, I was.	They took my TV.

Vocabulary

Listen. Repeat. Circle and write new words.

arrive

happen

report

crime

police

witness

van

robbed = took

Grammar Talk:
Past-Tense Statements with Regular and Irregular Verbs

Regular Verbs		Negative = did not	(didn't)	
I	work**ed**.	I	**did not**	(**didn't**)	work.
He	wait**ed**.	He	**did not**	(**didn't**)	wait.
She	walk**ed**.	She	**did not**	(**didn't**)	walk.
You	play**ed**.	You	**did not**	(**didn't**)	play.
We	arrive**d**.	We	**did not**	(**didn't**)	arrive.
They	studi**ed**.	They	**did not**	(**didn't**)	study.

What letters are used to make the past tense in regular verbs?
Some verbs have irregular forms. They do not use the -ed ending
to show past tense.

I **do** my homework every day.	I **did** my homework last night.
Mrs. Caruso often **sees** Sara.	Mrs. Caruso **saw** the burglar.
I **have** my photos in an album now.	I **had** my photos in a box before.
She **goes** home at 10:00 every night.	She **went** home at 10:00 last night.
We always **take** our lunch to work.	We **took** our lunch to work Friday.
He **wears** blue jeans most days.	He **wore** black pants yesterday.

Pronunciation Target • Past-Tense Ending Sounds

🎧 *Listen to your teacher or the audio.*

Sara worked.   The police arrived.   Mrs. Caruso waited.

Activity A Write about Sara's burglary. Write three sentences. Use the past tense.

1. She (arrive) _____arrived_____ home at _____10:00_____ .

2. She (call) _____ the _____ .

3. She (talk) _____ to _____ .

4. Her neighbor (see) _____ a _____ .

> insurance agent
> police officer
> report number

Activity B Read the Burglary Report Form. Use the questions below to role-play with your partner. Partner A is an insurance agent asking the questions. Partner B is Sara.

POLICE DEPARTMENT, CITY OF SACRAMENTO, CA		
Burglary Report No. *29657*	Date of Burglary *7/8/04*	Time of Crime *9:30-10:00 p.m.*
Name *Sara Morgan*	Items Missing	
Address *182 Clare Avenue #2 Sacramento, CA 95818*	Computer Model/ID Number *GBH-22445* TV Model/ID Number *Starline - 365HB*	
Phone No. *555-0460*	VCR Model/ID Number *Starline - 498CD*	
Witness *Lucy Caruso, 182 Clare Avenue #5 555-1197*	Officer *Roberta Collins*	

1. When did the burglary happen?
2. What things did the burglar take?
3. Where did the burglary happen?
4. Who was the police officer?
5. What was the report number?
6. Did a witness see the burglar?

TASK 2 Fill Out a Report

Talk to your partner or group about a burglary you know about. Answer the questions in Activity B.

One Step Up
Write a report in your notebook about the burglary.

Wanted!

◆ Describe people
◆ Ask questions in the past tense

Can you describe a person?

describe
suspect
wanted

◆ **Reading Tip** Flyers with pictures of people sometimes give a description of the person. Read this flyer. Look for the words that describe the person.

WANTED!

This person is a suspect in several burglaries in this neighborhood. If you see him, call the police at 555-3467.

Description:
Male, white, 20-30 years old
5'9"-6' tall
160-180 pounds
blond hair
brown eyes
mustache

It's him!

Talk or Write

1. Did the suspect have black hair?
2. Did he have a mustache?
3. Did he wear glasses?

Class Chat Choose a class "burglar." Describe a person in your class.

What did he look like?

He was tall and thin.

Vocabulary

Listen. Repeat. Circle and write new words.

describe

description

strange

beard

glasses

mustache

short

tall

heavy

thin

Name	What colors were his/her clothes?	What did he/she look like?
Marta	His shirt was blue. His pants were tan.	He was tall and thin.

Grammar Talk: Past-tense Questions with *Be*

Question Word	Verb	Subject		Answer
	Were	you	at home last night?	Yes, I was.
				No, I was not (wasn't).
Where	**were**	you	last night?	I was at home.

Remember questions with be *in the present tense? How are these the same?*

Past-tense Questions with Other Verbs

Question Word	Helping Verb	Subject	Main Verb	Answer
	Did	you	**lock** the door?	Yes, I did.
				No, I did not. (didn't)
When	**did**	you	**call** the police?	I called them last night.

What word shows past tense? What happens to the main verb in the past tense?

Activity A   You were in a store. You saw a woman take jewelry. She didn't pay for it. She ran from the store. The police officer needs information. Write answers to his questions.

1. Was she thin or heavy? <u>She was thin.</u>

2. What color were her eyes? _____

3. What kind of clothes did she wear? _____

4. Did she wear glasses? _____

5. When did she leave the store? _____

Activity B   Make questions about Sara's day. Use the time line. Ask and answer the questions with your partner.

When did Sara get up?

She got up at 6.

One Step Up
Make a time line of your day yesterday. Tell your class about your day.

6:00 A.M.	8:30 A.M.	12 Noon	1–9 P.M.	10 P.M.	10:30 P.M.	11:30 P.M.
Got up.	Started school.	Ate lunch.	Worked at job.	Arrived home.	Talked to police.	Went to bed.

⭐ **In the US**   Neighborhood Watch Programs

Many people help their neighbors.
They watch the homes in their neighborhood.
They tell their neighbors about strangers.

☛ **Compare Cultures**

How did you help your
neighbors in your home country?

program

strangers

watch

 TASK 3 Describe a Person

Find pictures of people in a magazine. Choose one of the people as the suspect in a burglary. Write five questions about the person. Ask your partner the questions.

Home Safety Packet

Plan, prepare, and make a Home Safety Packet.

Get Ready

Think about the things in your home. Do you have a TV? Do you have a car? Do you have information at home about the things you buy?

Do the Work

Use the Home Inventory form your teacher gives you. Write a list of the important things you have. Put a copy in your desk at home. Think about how you protect your things. Write in your notebook.

HOME INVENTORY

Name		Brand/Model	
Car			
Bicycle			
Electronics:			
TV			
VCR			
CD Player			
Jewelry			

Present Your Project

With your group, talk about your Home Inventory. How important are these things to you? Is there something that is not on the list? Why? Talk about how you protect your things. With your group, write what to do to protect your things. Share your group's ideas with the class. Make a class list of ideas.

✎ **Writing Extension** Who has keys to your home? Who has keys to your car? Write sentences.

✁💻 **Technology Extra**
Make a table on the computer. Type or write your home inventory.

Succeeding at School

Talking to Teachers

Home
1

Community
2

Work/School
3

◆ **Vocabulary** School words • Report cards • After-school activities

◆ **Language** Possessive adjectives • Compound sentences with *and* • Future tense with *going to*

◆ **Pronunciation** Long and short *o* sounds

◆ **Culture** Parent participation in schools

basketball
evening
ice cream shop
piano
sports

Monday–Friday, 7:00 A.M.

Monday–Friday, 8:30 A.M.

Monday–Thursday, 4:00 P.M.

Monday, Wednesday, Thursday, 5:30–8:00 P.M.

Tuesday, 6:00 P.M.

Monday–Thursday, 11:00 P.M.

What do your children do after school?
What do you do after school?

Thuy's daughter, Minh, is in high school.
Minh has activities after school.
She works three evenings a week.

Remember?

activity

Think and Talk

1. What do you see?
2. Are you busy? Are your children busy? Explain your answer.

What's Your Opinion? Are outside activities as important as school?

❑ Always   ❑ Sometimes   ❑ Never

Picture Dictionary   Listen. Repeat. Circle new words. Write the words.

| homework/ study | | work | | tired | | busy |

Gather Your Thoughts   What do you do during the week?

Make an idea map. Write what you do. Here's an example.

What do you do during the week?

Before School
1. _Make breakfast for my family._
2. _____
_____
3. _____
_____

After School
1. _Go shopping._
_____
2. _____
_____
3. _____
_____

What's the Problem?   How are your children doing in school? How are you doing in school? Think or talk with a partner.

Idiom Watch!

How are you doing?

Setting Goals   Check ✔ your school goals.

❏ **1.** Know when to talk to your teacher or your child's teacher.

❏ **2.** Go to a school meeting.

❏ **3.** Read a report card.

❏ **4.** Decide what things in your life are important.

❏ **5.** Change your schedule.

❏ **6.** Another goal: _____

Reading a Report Card

◆ Read a report card
◆ Use possessive adjectives

| attitude |
| code |
| conduct |
| habit |
| quarter |
| report card (grade card) |

What can you learn from a report card?

◆ **Reading Tip** Read the words in **bold** first.

RIVERTON HIGH SCHOOL
Report Card 2003-2004

Student Name: Le, Minh   Grade: 10
SSN: 999-24-9138

Period	Class	Teacher	Code	Quarter 1	Quarter 2	Quarter 3	Quarter 4
1	Geometry	Mr. Albers	4, 5, 6	A	B-	D+	
2	P.E.	Ms. King	3	A	A-	B-	
3	Biology	Mr. Kenyon	1, 5	B-	C+	C-	
4	World History	Mr. Marshall	1	B+	B	C+	
5	English	Ms. Evans	3, 6	B+	B	C-	
6	Spanish	Ms. Larson	5	A	B	B-	

Codes: 1 = good attitude   2 = shows improvement
3 = good class conduct   4 = call the teacher for an appointment
5 = poor study habits   6 = late for classes

Additional Comments:

Thuy reads Minh's report card from school.

Talk or Write

1. How often does Thuy see Minh's grades?
2. How did Minh do in Quarter 3?
3. Is Minh doing well in school? How do you know?

Remember?

appointment

improvement

Class Chat What subjects did you study in school? What subjects do your children study in school? Walk around. Ask questions. Write answers in your chart.

What subjects did you study in school?

I studied Russian, math, and science.

Name	What subjects did you study in school?	What subjects do your children study?
Petra	I studied Russian, math, and science.	They study history, English, and science.

Vocabulary

Listen. Repeat. Circle and write new words.

subject

English

history

math (geometry)

physical education (P.E.)

science (biology)

Spanish

Grammar Talk: Possessive Adjectives (Review)

Subject Pronoun	Possessive Adjective	
I	my	I like **my** new teacher.
you	your	**You** can open **your** book now.
he, she, it	his, her, its	**She** does **her** homework every night.
we	our	**We** have **our** class picnic on Friday.
you	your	Do **you** have **your** English book?
they	their	**They** have **their** lunch at noon.

Minh's basketball game is on Friday. = **Her** basketball game is on Friday.

What follows a possessive adjective? What does a possessive adjective tell you?

Activity A Look at the report card on page 96 to answer the questions. Use possessive pronouns.

1. What is Mr. Albers's class? <u>His class is Geometry.</u>

2. What's the name of the school? <u>Its name is Riverton High School.</u>

3. What are Ms. King's and Mr. Kenyon's classes? _____

4. What period is Ms. Evans's class? _____

5. Who is Minh's geometry teacher? _____

Activity B   Complete the conversation. Use the words in the box.

her	your	his	✔ my	your

Thuy: Hello. Mr. Albers?

Mr. Albers: Yes.

Thuy: This is Thuy Le. _____ My _____ daughter, Minh, is in
1
_____ geometry class.
2

Mr. Albers: Yes, Mrs. Le. I want to talk to you about _____ school
3
work.

Thuy: Is 5:30 on Thursday OK?

Mr. Albers: My son plays soccer on Thursday. _____ game starts at
4
5:30. But Wednesday is OK.

Thuy: Wednesday at 5:30 is fine.

Mr. Albers: Is _____ husband coming too?
5

Thuy: No. He's working late that night.

Mr. Albers: OK. See you Wednesday. Good-bye.

Thuy: Good-bye.

Practice the conversation with your partner.

TASK 1   Your School Information

What grades are your children in? Who are their teachers?
What class are you in? Who is your teacher?

Name	Grade/Level	Teacher's Name

One Step Up
Talk to a partner. Partner A is a teacher. Partner B is a student. Make an appointment with the teacher.

Making Decisions

◆ Decide what's most important
◆ Make compound sentences with *and*

How busy are your children? How busy are you?

◆ **Listening Tip** 🎧 Look at the questions below the picture. Then listen to the conversation between Thuy and her sister-in-law. Listen to your teacher or the audio. You can read the words on page 120.

> fix breakfast =
> make breakfast
>
> after
> before
> too many

Talk or Write

1. Why is Thuy worried about her daughter?
2. Who does Thuy want to talk to?
3. What activities does Minh have after school?
4. What does Minh do before school?

What's Your Opinion? Is it good to be busy? Explain your answer.

Class Chat Walk around. Ask questions. Write answers in your chart.

What activities do your children have after school?

Soccer and a job.

Name	What activities do you or your children have after school?	What time do you/ they go to bed?
Yuri	Soccer and a job.	9 p.m.

Activity A **Class Chat Follow-Up** Look at your Class Chat chart. Write sentences in your notebook.

<u>Yuri plays soccer and has a job after school. He goes to bed at 9 p.m.</u>

Vocabulary

Listen. Repeat. Circle and write new words.

basketball

piano

soccer

sports

Remember?

practice

schedule

Grammar Talk: Compound Sentences with *And*

Thuy starts work at 6:00 A.M. Minh starts school at 8:00 A.M.

Thuy starts work at 6:00 A.M., **and** Minh starts school at 8:00 A.M.

Thuy gets home at 5:00 P.M. Minh gets home at 8:00 P.M.

Thuy gets home at 5:00 P.M., **and** Minh gets home at 8:00 P.M.

What word makes two sentences into one sentence? What do you see before the word and *in these sentences?*

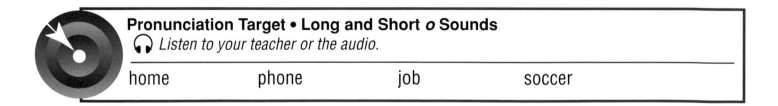

Pronunciation Target • Long and Short *o* Sounds

🎧 *Listen to your teacher or the audio.*

home   phone   job   soccer

Activity B   What did Thuy and Minh do last Saturday?
Talk and write.

Name	Day	9:00–11:00	11:00–12:00	1:00–3:00	4:00–6:00	6:00–9:00
Minh	Saturday	play soccer	homework	job	job	baby-sit
Thuy	Saturday	watch soccer	visit a friend	clean house	help kids study	eat out

1. 9:00–11:00   _Minh played soccer, and Thuy watched._

2. 11:00–12:00 _____

3. 1:00–3:00   _____

4. 4:00–6:00   _____

5. 6:00–9:00   _____

Activity C   Make a list of Minh's activities in order of
importance. Number 1 is most important.

baby-sit	homework	school	work at the ice cream shop
basketball	piano lessons	soccer	help other children

1. _____   **5.** _____

2. _____   **6.** _____

3. _____   **7.** _____

4. _____   **8.** _____

Talk with your partner. Do you and your partner agree?

TASK 2   Make an Activities Chart
List your activities in order of importance. Make a chart.

One Step Up
Show your chart to the class.
Talk about your answers.

Parent-Teacher Meeting

◆ Plan for school success
◆ Use *going to* to talk about the future

fall asleep

surprised

turn in

When do you need to talk to a teacher?

◆ **Reading Tip** Look at the picture before you read. Do you know what they are talking about?

Talking to the Teacher

Thuy has a meeting with Minh's geometry teacher, Mr. Albers. He tells Thuy these things. Minh had good grades in September, and she was a good student.

Now things are different. Minh is often late to class, and she has ten absences.

Sometimes Minh falls asleep in class, and she doesn't turn in her homework on time.

Thuy is surprised. Minh needs to pass this class. Thuy is going to talk with her. They are going to make changes in Minh's life.

Talk or Write

1. Who did Thuy have a meeting with?
2. How were Minh's grades in September?
3. Why is Minh having problems in class now?

Class Chat Walk around. Ask questions. Write answers in your chart.

Name	What can you do to succeed at school?
Isabel	I can get to school on time. I can take a different bus.

Then write sentences in your notebook.

To succeed in school, Isabel can get to school on time.

Vocabulary

Listen. Repeat. Circle and write new words.

counselor

principal

check

fail

pass

succeed

Grammar Talk: Future Tense with *Going to*

Subject	Be	Going to	Main Verb (Base Form)	
I	**am**	**going to**	check	my daughter's homework.
You	**are**	**going to**	call	the principal.
He/She	**is**	**going to**	talk	to Minh.
We/They	**are**	**going to**	meet	with the counselor.

What verb comes before going to? *What verb* <u>form</u> *follows* going to?
Remember: To make a question with a form of be, *put it in front of the subject.*
  Thuy is *going to talk to Minh.*   Is *Thuy going to talk to Minh?*

Activity A Use words from each box to write sentences in your notebook.

I	am going to	talk to my children.
My son	are going to	study English.
My daughters	is going to	go to bed on time.
My children		stay home at night.

I am going to study English.

Activity B What are people in your family going to do this weekend? Write sentences with *and*.

1. <u>I'm going to go to the library, and my son is going to play basketball.</u>

2. _____

3. _____

4. _____

5. _____

6. _____

In the US   Parents and Schools

Teachers in the US like to talk to parents about their children. Sometimes they write notes to the parents, and sometimes they call the parents. Parents need to call teachers to see how their children are doing.

Principals, counselors, teachers, and parents work together to help children succeed.

☛ **Compare Cultures**

How do parents and teachers work together in your home country? Do they talk about the children? When? Where? Talk with your group.

TASK 3 Success Planning Chart

What will it take for you to succeed in school?

1. In your group, make a list of things you can do to succeed in school.

2. Find pictures to show how you can succeed. Make a poster with your group. Put the poster on the wall of your classroom.

Make a School Information Chart

Do these things to make a School Information Chart.

Get Ready

Do these things:

1. Find the address and phone numbers for your school or your child's school.
2. Who are the teachers for your family?
3. Who has these jobs at your (or your child's) school:
   - Principal
   - Vice-Principal
   - Counselor

Do the Work

Complete the chart from your teacher with your information. Practice calling your school or your child's school. Write a note to your teacher or your child's teacher.

absent = not in class

Sample phone call

"Hello. My name's _____,
                     your name

and I'm _____'s
          your child's name

_____. He's/she's in
     parent or guardian

_____'s class."
     teacher's name

"My child will be absent today. He/she is sick."

OR

"My child will be late today. He/she will be at school at _____."
                              time

Sample note

Please excuse my _____,
                     son/daughter

_____.
     your child's name

She was home on _____
                     day and date

because she had _____
     _____.
     a cold/a doctor's appointment, etc.

Sincerely,

_____ Date _____
     your signature

Present Your Project

Talk to your group or the class about your chart.

Technology Extra

Make a copy of your chart for your school on the photocopier.
Put the chart on the wall in your classroom.

One Step Up

Invite school employees to class to talk about their jobs. Ask questions and make a new chart.

I Want a Good Job!

Improving Your Skills

Work/School
1

Home
2

Community
3

◆ **Vocabulary** Employment words • Educational opportunities

◆ **Language** *Can* and *can't* • Compound sentences with *but*
   • *A, an, the*

◆ **Pronunciation** Long and short *u* sounds

◆ **Culture** Education can increase income

Do you have the job you want?

Cesar works at Best Computer Factory. Pilar volunteers at a library. They like their work, but they are ready for more responsibility.

Think and Talk

1. What's the problem?
2. Who tells you about job opportunities?

apply
award
factory
library
qualified
volunteer

Gather Your Thoughts
Who tells you how you're doing? Make an idea map. Here's an example.

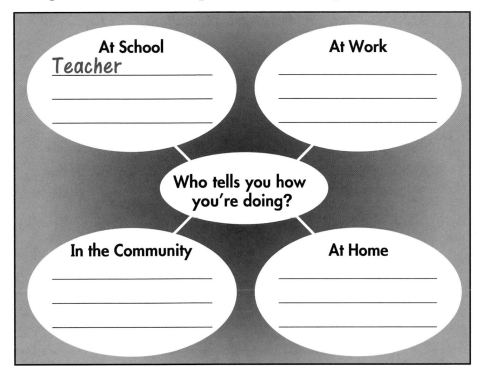

At School
Teacher
_____
_____

At Work
_____
_____
_____

Who tells you how you're doing?

In the Community
_____
_____
_____

At Home
_____
_____
_____

Talk to a partner. Look at the circles. Talk about the people. Are their comments positive (+) or negative (–)? Which comments help you? Can negative comments sometimes help you?

Vocabulary

Listen. Repeat. Circle and write new words.

comment

opportunity

performance

promotion

review

supervisor

negative

positive

qualified

apply

promote

_____
your word

What's the Problem?
Is it easy to get more education or training in the US? Think or talk with a partner.

progress
training

Setting Goals
Check ✔ your career goals.

❏ 1. Understand a job performance review.

❏ 2. Talk to my supervisor about job opportunities.

❏ 3. Talk to my teacher about my ESL progress.

❏ 4. Make choices about my job.

❏ 5. Register for other education or training programs.

❏ 6. Another goal: _____

Good for You!

◆ Talk about job skills
◆ Use *can* and *can't*

Do you want a job with more responsibility?

attitude
experience

◆ **Reading Tip** Use the pictures to help you read.

Ms. Hunter is Cesar's supervisor. She congratulates him on his award for Employee of the Month. Cesar does very good work and is on time every day. He helps the other workers. People like to work with him.

Ms. Hunter wants to give Cesar a promotion. The job has more responsibility and more money, but Cesar needs a high school diploma or GED for that job.

Pilar works at the library as a volunteer. She doesn't get money, but she gets experience. She's a good worker and very responsible. Everybody likes her good attitude. Now she's thinking about a job with pay at the library.

Cesar and Pilar are going to get married. They want to make more money.

Talk or Write

1. Why did Cesar get an award?
2. Can Cesar apply for a new job at the factory?
3. Why did Pilar get an award?

Class Chat Walk around. Ask questions. Write answers in your chart.

How can people get promotions?

They can be responsible workers.

Name	How can people get promotions?	What other things can they do?
Amy	They can be responsible workers.	They can arrive on time.

Activity A Class Chat Follow-Up Look at your chart. Write sentences in your notebook.

<u>People can get promotions by being responsible workers.</u>

Vocabulary

Listen. Repeat. Circle and write new words.

high school diploma

employee

GED

skill

responsibility

responsible

congratulate

solve

Grammar Talk: *Can* and *Can't*

Statement			Question	
I	**can/can't** apply for the job.	**Can/Can't**	I apply for the job?	
You	**can/can't** solve the problem.	**Can/Can't**	you solve the problem?	
He/she	**can/can't** speak English	**Can/Can't**	he/she speak English?	
We	**can/can't** do the job.	**Can/Can't**	we do the job?	
They	**can/can't** succeed.	**Can/Can't**	they succeed?	

Can *and* can't *let you talk about things you have the ability to do. What kind of word follows* can *or* can't *in a statement? What word changes place in a question? Talk to your teacher about these questions.*

Activity B Ask the students in your class. What can you do well at work? What can't you do well at work? What can you do well at school? What can't you do well at school? Make a list of what people in your class can do well.

I can speak Russian, but I can't speak Spanish.

Unit 8 Lesson 1 **109**

Activity C Look at Cesar's job review. Talk with your partner.

Best Computers Job Performance Review	Excellent	Good	Fair	Needs to Improve
Competencies and Job Skills				
On time for work	X	☐	☐	☐
Attendance	☐	X	☐	☐
Attitude	X	☐	☐	☐
Follows safety rules	X	☐	☐	☐
Machine A	☐	X	☐	☐
Machine B	☐	☐	X	☐
Machine C	X	☐	☐	☐

Employee: Cesar Rios

Position: Assembly Line   **SSN:** 999-73-6153

Comments: Cesar is a great employee. Other workers like to work with him. He needs a HS Diploma or GED.

Recommend for Promotion: ☒ Yes ☐ No

Can work:

Days ☒ Mon ☒ Tues ☒ Wed ☒ Thurs ☒ Fri ☒ Sat/Sun

Shift ☒ Day (7-3) ☐ Evening (3-11) ☐ Swing (11-7)

Signature: *Jackie Hunter*

Signature: **Cesar Rios**   Date: *7-8-04*

1. What can Cesar do well?
   What can't he do well?

2. When can Cesar work?
   When can't he work?

3. When can you work?
   When can you go to class?

4. When can't you work?
   When can't you go to class?

> competencies = things you do well
> excellent/good = well
> fair = OK
> needs to improve = not well
> shift = hours you work

TASK 1 List Your Skills

What jobs can you do? What other skills do you have? Interview
your partner. Make a chart for your group.

Name	Jobs	Skills
Olga	Cook	Speak English and Spanish.

The reporter from your group can give the information to the class.

Technology Extra
Make a chart on the computer. Use the information from the students
in the class. The title of the chart is **Our Jobs and Our Skills.**

Planning a Future

◆ Talk about future goals
◆ Use compound sentences with *but*

What are your plans for the future?

deserve

distance learning

◆ **Listening Tip** 🎧 You don't need to understand every word, but you need to understand the main idea. Listen to your teacher or the audio. You can read the words on page 120.

Idiom Watch!
Hey!

Talk or Write

1. What jobs are Cesar and Pilar thinking about?
2. What idea does Pilar have?
3. In what two places can they study?
4. What do you know about distance learning? What do you want to know?

What's Your Opinion? Is it better to study in class or at home?

Class Chat Cesar and Pilar want different jobs. What job(s) do you have? What job(s) do you want? Walk around. Ask questions. Write answers in your chart.

Vocabulary

Listen. Repeat. Circle and write new words.

congratulations

deserve

distance learning

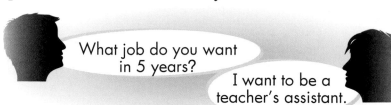

What job do you want in 5 years?

I want to be a teacher's assistant.

Name	What job do you want in five years?	What are the requirements for that job?
Galina	I want to teach.	I need to pass an English test.

Activity A **Class Chat Follow-Up** Look at your Class Chat chart. Write sentences in your notebook.

<u>Galina wants to teach, but she needs to pass an English test.</u>

Grammar Talk: Compound Sentences with *But*

Cesar wants a supervisor job, **but** he needs a high school diploma.

He likes his company, **but** he wants a different job there.

What punctuation mark is used before but? *Talk to your teacher.*

Pronunciation Target • Long and Short *u* Sounds

🎧 *Listen to your teacher or the audio.*

use   computer   us   but

Activity B Write the correct letter to complete the sentence.

__b__ 1. My son wants good grades,   a. but she needs a job with pay.

_____ 2. I want to read to my children,   b. but he watches too much TV.

_____ 3. I want to go to work today,   c. but I can't read English.

_____ 4. Pilar likes her volunteer job,   d. but I have a bad cold.

Activity C   Talk to your partner. What do you have, want, need, and like? What's the problem? Use *but* to write one sentence for each verb.

I have a computer at home. I don't know how to use it.

1. _I have a computer at home, but I don't know how to use it._

2. _____

3. _____

4. _____

5. _____

TASK 2   Make a Goals Chart

Work in a group. Think about the future.

What do you want to do?   OR   What do you want to be?

What do you need to do to make that happen?

Read the questions with a partner. Complete the chart.

One Step Up

Think about five years from now. Where do you want to be? What job do you want to have? Use the computer and write your future address and job.

	I can	I want to	I need to	My Goals
School	speak 3 languages	go to college	finish high school	I want to go to college, but I need to finish high school.
Work				
Family				
Community				

Talk to your partner. Tell him or her your information. Tell someone else in your group about your partner.

Distance Learning

- ◆ Read flyers
- ◆ Use *a, an, the*

Is distance learning a good idea for you?

◆ **Reading Tip** Look for specific information—times and dates—when you read a poster or a flyer.

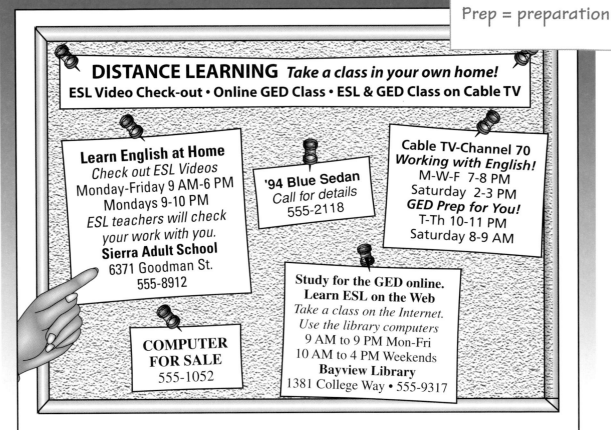

DISTANCE LEARNING *Take a class in your own home!*
ESL Video Check-out • Online GED Class • ESL & GED Class on Cable TV

Learn English at Home
Check out ESL Videos
Monday-Friday 9 AM-6 PM
Mondays 9-10 PM
*ESL teachers will check
your work with you.*
Sierra Adult School
6371 Goodman St.
555-8912

'94 Blue Sedan
Call for details
555-2118

Cable TV-Channel 70
Working with English!
M-W-F 7-8 PM
Saturday 2-3 PM
GED Prep for You!
T-Th 10-11 PM
Saturday 8-9 AM

Study for the GED online.
Learn ESL on the Web
Take a class on the Internet.
Use the library computers
9 AM to 9 PM Mon-Fri
10 AM to 4 PM Weekends
Bayview Library
1381 College Way • 555-9317

**COMPUTER
FOR SALE**
555-1052

Pilar is showing these flyers about distance learning to Cesar.

Talk or Write

1. Where can Cesar and Pilar take a distance-learning class?
2. What classes can Cesar and Pilar take?
3. What are two ways that Cesar can study for the GED?
4. What are three ways that Pilar can study ESL?

Class Chat   Walk around. Ask questions. Write answers in your chart.

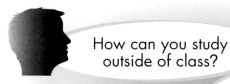

How can you study outside of class?

I can watch a video.

Vocabulary

Listen. Repeat. Circle and write new words.

check out

cable TV

Internet

online

tape

video

web

Name	How can you study outside of class?	When do you like to study?
Andres	I can watch a video.	From 10:00-11:00 p.m.

Grammar Talk: A, An, The

I want to check out **a** video.	I'm going to take **an** Internet course.
Do you need **an** ESL video?	Yes, I need **the** video for **the** first three lessons.

What letter follows a? *What letter follows* an?
Use a *and* an *with one person, place, or thing.*
Use the *with one or more people, places, or things.*
A *or an refers to any singular item.* The *refers to a specific item or items.*

Activity A   Can you always get to your ESL class? Look at the pictures. Complete the sentence: I wanted to go to class, but _____

1. _I wanted to go to class, but my car had a flat tire._

2. _____

3. _____

Activity B   Complete the sentences. Use *a*, *an*, or *the*.

Cesar goes to _____*the*_____ downtown library with Pilar. He sees
1

_____ flyers about distance-learning programs. He wants more
2

information. Pilar asks about _____ ESL videos. She wants to improve
3

her English, but there isn't _____ adult school near her home. Cesar
4

wants to apply for _____ supervisor job at his company, but
5

he needs _____ high school diploma or GED. He can attend
6

_____ evening high school class, or he can use _____
7   8

computer from the library to study online.

In the US   Education Can Increase Income

Annual US Household Average Income by Level of Education	
Education	**Average Income**
9th to 12th grade	$22,753
High School Diploma	$36,722
Some College	$44,449
College Degree	$71,437
Source: US Census Bureau 2002	

People in the US can get a job with a high school diploma.
But more training and education often means more income.
Many companies offer training for their employees.

Most people take classes at school. Some people
take distance-learning classes on TV or on the
Internet. People of all ages can learn new skills.

> income
>
> increase = make bigger

TASK 3   Community Places for Education

Where can you get the job skills you need? Read information
about your school. Does your school offer a distance-learning
program? Find other adult classes in your city. Make a list.

Your Goals

Do these things to make a goals time line and a resume.

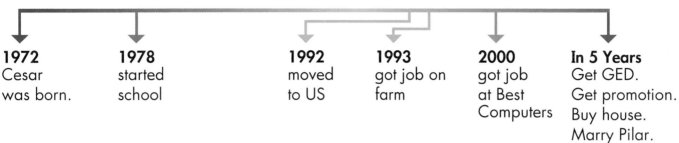

1972
Cesar
was born.

1978
started
school

1992
moved
to US

1993
got job on
farm

2000
got job
at Best
Computers

In 5 Years
Get GED.
Get promotion.
Buy house.
Marry Pilar.

Get Ready

Do these things:

- Look at Cesar's time line.
- Make a time line of the important events and goals in **your** life.
- Give your time line to your partner.
- Talk about the important events in your life.
- Tell about your goals and how you're going to reach them.

Do the Work

- Write a simple resume.
- Use the information from your time line.
- Look at this example.

Cesar Rios

EDUCATION	WORK EXPERIENCE
Rafael Reyes Escuela Secundaria	Clerk, Banco Nacional
Guadalajara, Mexico 1987-89	Monterey, Mexico 1989-1991

Present Your Project

Talk to your group or the class about your time line.

What events were very important?

Tell about your goals. Give your resume to your class.

Technology Extra

Write your resume on the computer. Make copies for the students in your class.

Listening Scripts

Warm-Up Unit
Are You Ready?

Lesson 2, page 15

Teacher: Welcome to English class, Tomas. Where are you from?

Tomas: I'm from Chile. Teacher, I need a pencil.

Teacher: Here's one. Bring a pencil tomorrow. And my name is Pat Allen.

Tomas: Hello, Mr. Allen.

Teacher: Now class, ready to write? OK, open your books. Do exercise A with your partners. Answer the questions.

Page 16

Pronunciation Target
Syllable Stress
late   STU dent   di REC tions

Page 20
Activity A
1. How much are two notebooks? Two notebooks are $6.00.
2. How much are four pens? Four pens are $8.00.
3. How much are 10 pencils? Ten pencils are $2.00.
4. How much is the paper? The paper is $2.50.

Activity B

Tomas: I need to buy school supplies.

Clerk: What supplies do you need?

Tomas: I need a notebook and a dictionary.

Clerk: English or Spanish-English?

Tomas: Spanish-English, please.

Clerk: That's $8.45.

Tomas: OK. Here's $10.00.

Clerk: And $1.55 in change.

Unit 1
My Life Is Changing!

Lesson 2, page 27

Nassim: Lusala, I'm worried. My parents need help.

Lusala: They need to live here. What's the problem?

Nassim: This apartment is small with only two bedrooms.

Lusala: Apartments with three bedrooms in this neighborhood are expensive.

Nassim: Maybe I need a part-time job.

Lusala: No problem for you, Nassim! Your English is good.

Page 28

Pronunciation Target
Is Nassim at home? Yes, she is.

Unit 2
I Need to Plan a Party

Page 37

Pronunciation Target
wants
likes
writes
needs
agrees
ends

Lesson 3, page 42

Boris: Happy birthday, Pavel! This is a special cake for you.

Yelena: Oh, no! Here comes the rain! Boris, what can we do?

Boris: Let's go to the porch.

Rosa: Good idea. We can have the party there.

Yelena: Boris, take the cake. I'll take the presents.

Rosa: Kids, run to the porch.

Page 43

Pronunciation Target
rain
cake

favor
plan
at
glad

Page 44
Activity B

Miguel: Hello, Yelena. I am Miguel and this is Sylvia. We are Ben's parents.

Yelena: It's nice to meet you, Miguel and Sylvia. This is my husband, Boris.

Miguel: Hi, Boris. Thank you for inviting Ben to the party.

Boris: It's nice to have Ben here. Pavel, thank Ben for his present.

Pavel: Thanks for the backpack, Ben. It's great!

Ben: I'm glad you like it. Thanks for the cake. Mom, Pavel's dad makes great cakes.

Sylvia: Really? I need to call you, Boris. I need a cake for a church meeting next week.

Unit 3
How Do You Feel?

Lesson 2, page 51

Receptionist: Dr. Lee's office.

Jim: Hello, this is Jim Martin. I need an appointment with the doctor.

Receptionist: What's the problem, Mr. Martin?

Jim: I feel sick. My throat hurts, and I have a bad headache.

Receptionist: Do you have a fever?

Jim: Yes, my temperature's 101 degrees.

Receptionist: OK. The doctor can see you tomorrow, June 10, at 3:00 P.M.

Jim: Tomorrow at 3:00. Thank you.

Page 55

Pronunciation Target

Is your appointment at 3:00 P.M.?
When is your appointment?

Unit 4
I Need a Budget!

Lesson 2, page 63

Ramon: Mr. Martin, I need to talk to you. I want to work more hours at the restaurant.

Mr. Martin: I'm sorry, Ramon. First you need to improve your service, your clothes, and your English.

Ramon: I'm studying English at school now.

Mr. Martin: That's good. But you speak only Spanish to the other workers.

Ramon: I'm trying to help them with their jobs.

Mr. Martin: You need to help the customers first. Those people need their bill. Remember—happy customers give good tips!

Ramon: OK, you're right. Thanks for the advice. I know I can do a better job.

Page 64

Pronunciation Target

cheap
e-mail
need
rent
spend
expensive

Page 68

Activity A

Ramon: I need to return these shirts.

Salesperson: What's the problem?

Ramon: They don't fit well. Is that shirt on sale?

Salesperson: No, it isn't. This shirt is on sale.

Ramon: Good! I need a medium in black.

Salesperson: OK. Anything else?

Ramon: No, thanks. That's it for today.

Unit 5
What's for Dinner?

Page 73

Pronunciation Target

The store has apples, eggs, bananas, and corn on sale.

Lesson 3, page 78

Listen. Miyako and her friends are at school.

Maria: It's lunch time! We're going to eat. Come with us.

Miyako: To where?

Maria: To Hamburger Hut or Tacos to Go for a fast lunch.

Miyako: Thanks, but I have my lunch today. I'm going to eat in the cafeteria.

Maria: Come on! The burgers and fries are really good.

Miyako: I know, but I'm trying to eat well and save money.

Maria: OK. See you in English class.

Page 80
Activity A

People in the US are very busy. They often don't have time to buy or cook food. At school or at work they are far from home. Fast food is popular. But there are problems with fast food. It often has a lot of fat, salt, or sugar. Too much fat, salt, and sugar are bad for people's health. Some fast-food restaurants are changing. Now they have salads or other healthy foods. Small changes in food choices can make big health differences.

Activity B

Clerk: Welcome to Hamburger Hut. Your order, please.

Maria: I'd like Fast Meal Number 3. Are there fries with that?

Clerk: Yes, there are. And to drink? Soda or coffee?

Maria: Orange soda, please.

Clerk: For here or to go?

Maria: To go.

Clerk: Okay, that's $4.25.

Unit 6
Call the Police!

Page 85

Pronunciation Target

quiet
night
crime
window
missing
important

Lesson 2, page 87

Officer Collins: Ms. Morgan, we need you to fill out a police report. Please tell us what happened first.

Sara: I came home about 10:00 P.M. When I arrived at the door, it was open.

Officer Collins: Then what happened?

Sara: I went inside, looked around, and I saw this mess!

Officer Collins: And then? Was anything missing?

Sara: Yes, several things—a computer, a TV, and a VCR.

Officer Collins: Did your neighbors see anything?

Sara: Yes, my neighbor, Mrs. Caruso, saw a man about 9:50 P.M. He put a TV in his van.

Page 88

Pronunciation Target

Sara worked. The police arrived. Mrs. Caruso waited.

Unit 7
Succeeding at School

Lesson 2, page 99

Thuy: Minh is always tired. Her school gives a lot of homework. I want to talk to the principal.

Karen: Maybe she has too many classes. Her counselor can change her schedule.

Thuy: Look at her report card.

Karen: Oh, Thuy. Her grades are not good this quarter. What is happening?

Thuy: Well, Minh is very busy this year. She has school, a job, basketball, soccer, and piano.

Karen: And does she help your other children get ready for school in the morning?

Thuy: Yes, Karl and I start work at 6 A.M. I need her to fix breakfast for the kids.

Karen: I understand why she's tired all the time.

Page 100

Pronunciation Target

home
phone
job
soccer

Unit 8
I Want a Good Job!

Lesson 2, page 111

Pilar: Congratulations, honey, on your award. You deserved it.

Cesar: You deserved your award too, Pilar. Let's celebrate our future!

Pilar: Are you thinking about the supervisor job?

Cesar: Yes, but I need a high school diploma or my GED.

Pilar: That's like me. The volunteer work was good experience, and now I want a clerk job with pay. But I still need to study more English.

Cesar: It's not easy to work and study. We need time for us too.

Pilar: Hey! I read a flyer at the library about learning at home. It's called distance learning.

Cesar: Great! Let's look at it. Maybe we can learn at home together.

Page 112

Pronunciation Target

use
computer
us
but

The US

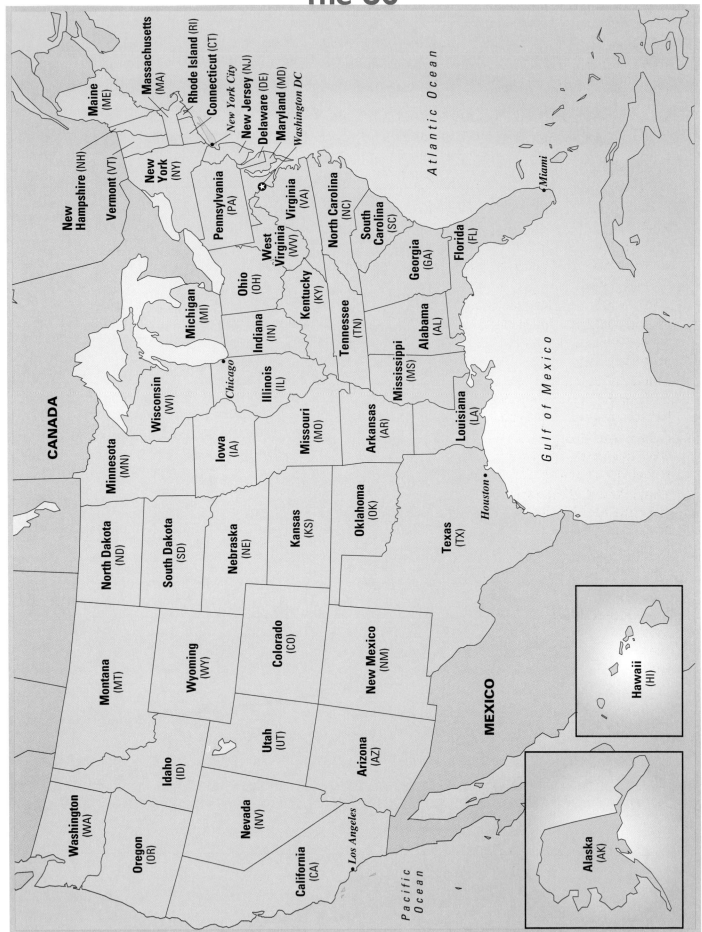

The World

Arctic
Ocean

Canada

North America

North
Pacific Ocean

North
Atlantic Ocean

United States

Mexico   Cuba

Central   Jamaica   Dominican Republic
America   Belize   Puerto Rico
Guatemala   Honduras   Haiti
El Salvador
Nicaragua   Guyana
Costa Rica   Venezuela   Suriname
Panama   Colombia
Ecuador

South America

Peru   Brazil
Bolivia

South
Pacific Ocean   Chile   Paraguay

Uruguay

Argentina

South
Atlantic Ocean

Europe

Ukraine

Russia

Asia

China

North
Korea

Japan

South
Korea

India

North
Pacific Ocean

Africa

Vietnam   Philippines

Indian Ocean

Australia

Antarctica

Alphabet and Numbers

The Alphabet

A	B	C	D	E	F	G	H	I	J	K	L	M
A	*B*	*C*	*D*	*E*	*F*	*G*	*H*	*I*	*J*	*K*	*L*	*M*

N	O	P	Q	R	S	T	U	V	W	X	Y	Z
N	*O*	*P*	*Q*	*R*	*S*	*T*	*U*	*V*	*W*	*X*	*Y*	*Z*

a	b	c	d	e	f	g	h	i	j	k	l	m
a	*b*	*c*	*d*	*e*	*f*	*g*	*h*	*i*	*j*	*k*	*l*	*m*

n	o	p	q	r	s	t	u	v	w	x	y	z
n	*o*	*p*	*q*	*r*	*s*	*t*	*u*	*v*	*w*	*x*	*y*	*z*

Numbers

0	1	2	3	4	5	6	7	8	9	10
zero	one	two	three	four	five	six	seven	eight	nine	ten

11	12	13	14	15	16	17	18	19	20
eleven	twelve	thirteen	fourteen	fifteen	sixteen	seventeen	eighteen	nineteen	twenty

21	22	23	24	25	26	27	28	29	30
twenty-one	twenty-two	twenty-three	twenty-four	twenty-five	twenty-six	twenty-seven	twenty-eight	twenty-nine	thirty

40	50	60	70	80	90	100
forty	fifty	sixty	seventy	eighty	ninety	one hundred

200	300	400	500	600	700	800	900	1,000
two hundred	three hundred	four hundred	five hundred	six hundred	seven hundred	eight hundred	nine hundred	one thousand

Months and Days

Months	Abbreviations	Days	Abbreviations
1. January	Jan.	Sunday	Sun.
2. February	Feb.	Monday	Mon.
3. March	Mar.	Tuesday	Tues.
4. April	Apr.	Wednesday	Wed.
5. May	May.	Thursday	Thurs.
6. June	Jun.	Friday	Fri.
7. July	Jul.	Saturday	Sat.
8. August	Aug.		
9. September	Sept.		
10. October	Oct.		
11. November	Nov.		
12. December	Dec.		

August 2004

Sun.	Mon.	Tues.	Wed.	Thurs.	Fri.	Sat.
1	2	3	4	5	6	7
8	9	10	11	12	13	14
15	16	17	18	19	20	21
22	23	24	25	26	27	28
29	30	31				

US Holidays

Day	Date
New Year's Day	January 1
Martin Luther King Day	January 15*
Presidents' Day	third Monday in February
Memorial Day	May 30*
Independence Day	July 4
Labor Day	first Monday in September
Veterans Day	November 11
Thanksgiving	fourth Thursday in November
Christmas	December 25

* Observed on the closest Monday.

Verb Tense Review

present	past	present	past
buy	bought	see	saw
drive	drove	send	sent
eat	ate	spend	spent
fit	fit	take	took
give	gave	tell	told
make	made	wear	wore
ride	rode	write	wrote
run	ran		

Writing Checklist for Sentences

❏ **1.** <u>Did</u> I capitalize the first word of every sentence?

❏ **2.** Did I end every sentence with a period (.), question mark (?), or exclamation point (!)?

❏ **3.** Did I ~~used~~ use correct grammar?

❏ **4.** Did I check my ~~speling~~ spelling?

❏ **5.** *Is my handwriting neat and easy to read?*

Topics

Grammar and Pronunciation